SIX LITHUANIAN POETS

SIX LITHUANIAN POETS

Translated by Eugenijus Ališanka,
Kerry Shawn Keys, Medeinė Tribinevičius,
Laima Vincė and Jonas Zdanys

Edited and introduced by
Eugenijus Ališanka

PUBLICATIONS
2008

Published by Arc Publications
Nanholme Mill, Shaw Wood Road
Todmorden, OL14 6DA, UK
www.arcpublications.co.uk

Design by Tony Ward
Printed in Great Britain by
MPG Biddles, King's Lynn

ISBN: 978 1904614 85 2

The publishers are grateful to the authors and translators and,
in the case of previously published works, to their publishers
for allowing their poems to be included in this anthology.

Cover image: "The Iron Age" by Kazys Venclovas

Arc Publications gratefully acknowledges the financial support of
'Books from Lithuania' arising from the subsidy granted by the
Ministry of Culture of the Republic of Lithuania.

The publishers acknowledge financial assistance
from Arts Council England, Yorkshire

The 'New Voices from Europe and Beyond' anthology series is published in
co-operation with Literature Across Frontiers which receives support
from the Culture 2007 programme of the EU.

LITERATURE
ACROSS
FRONTIERS

**Arc Publications 'New Voices from Europe and Beyond'
Series Editor: Alexandra Büchler**

CONTENTS

DAIVA ČEPAUSKAITĖ
Translated by Jonas Zdanys, E.Ališanka and
Kerry Shawn Keys
Biography / 115

EUGENIJUS ALIŠANKA
Translated by the author and Kerry Shawn Keys
Biography / 137

SERIES EDITOR'S PREFACE

The present anthology is the fourth in a new and much-needed series which brings contemporary international poetry to English-language readers. It is not by accident that the tired old phrase about poetry being 'lost in translation' came out of an English-speaking environment, out of a tradition that has always felt remarkably uneasy about translation. Yet poetry can be, and *is*, 'found' in translation; in fact, any good translation *reinvents* the poetry of the original. We should never lose sight of the fact that translation is the outcome of a dialogue – between two cultures, two languages and two poetic traditions, between collective as well as individual imaginations – a dialogue conducted by two voices, those of the poet and of the translator, which are joined by a third participant in the process of interpretative reading.

It is this dialogue that is so important to writers in countries and regions where translation has always been an integral part of the literary environment and has played a role in the development of their literary tradition and poetics. Writing without having read poetry from other cultures would be unthinkable for the poets in the anthologies of this new series, many of whom are also accomplished translators, for, as well as considering poetry in translation part of their own literary background, they also regard it as an important source of inspiration.

While this series aims to keep a finger on the pulse of the here-and-now of contemporary poetry by presenting the work of a small number of contemporary poets, each collection, edited by a guest editor, has its own focus and rationale for the selection of the poets and poems.

The poets whose work is included in *Six Lithuanian Poets* were born in the 1960s, when Lithuania was part of the Soviet Union, and mostly started publishing after the country achieved independence in 1991. Unlike their predecessors, the poets of this generation are not concerned with political themes but rather with issues of aesthetics and existential quests. While each follows his / her unique path, they all share a penchant for experimentation and an ironic, post-modern perspective, following European literary trends rather than domestic poetic traditions.

I would like to thank those who made this edition possible and, above all, the translators and the poets themselves.

Alexandra Büchler

A SHORT INTRODUCTION TO
LITHUANIAN POETRY

The development of Lithuanian literature over the last two centuries has been closely connected with the history of the country and as a result has been often disrupted and held back. In the nineteenth century Lithuania was part of the tsarist Russian Empire and the natural evolution of its literature was obstructed by ideological and political restrictions. After the 1863 uprising against tsarist rule, the Lithuanian press and alphabet were banned and books could only be published in Cyrillic script. Lithuanian resistance took different forms during this period. Books were printed in Prussia (now the Kaliningrad region of the Russian Federation) and secretly brought to Lithuania by *knygnešiai*, book smugglers, who risked their lives and freedom. Most of the books published at that time, however, were educational in content. The beginnings of genuine literature were fostered by enlightened intellectuals, mostly priests, and literary life developed in the underground. The situation improved after 1904 when the ban on the Lithuanian press was lifted, but a more definite recovery of literature started only after 1918, when the country declared itself independent.

The following period – from 1918 to 1940 – was highly significant for Lithuanian writing. Immense changes took place during these two decades and literature could at last breathe freely. The opportunities to learn more about European culture and literature, the availability of a multitude of literary magazines, as well as changes in social life helped literature flourish. Along with poetry (a genre usually predominant in societies that lack the scope for free development), the Lithuanian novel emerged. In addition to realism, other modernist literary trends such as Symbolism, Futurism and neo-Romanticism were taking root on the domestic front. Urban themes also grew stronger and by the time the Second World War broke out, Lithuanian literature was capable of engaging in a dialogue with Europe.

Unfortunately, the Soviet invasion and occupation in 1941 interrupted and irrevocably damaged Lithuanian literary life: most writers emigrated to the West, others were repressed, exiled to Siberia, or forced to dance to the music of Stalinist ideology and aesthetics. Under such extreme political and ideological conditions, literature learned to speak in code while at the same time striving for authenticity and looking for loopholes in censorship. Of all genres, poetry enjoyed the greatest success. Poets mastered Aesop's language and created modern poetics that are still being developed today. As for prose, the situation was more difficult because narrative was more easily controlled ideologically; prose writers were required to adopt socialist realism which, because it had little to do with actual realism, used ideology to distort reality. Since historical and contemporary socio-political subjects were off limits, prose was most successful in its portrayal of peasant life and personal relationships, while remaining on the periphery of key social and political issues. Poetry, on the other hand, was more readily able to cross the line.

All of these interruptions have determined the way we look at Lithuanian literature today; we speak of the literature "before" and "after" to identify, resolve and reconcile what we have inherited from the period of occupation, and ask ourselves what we can learn from it and what we have to reject. Many authors whose books were published in thousands of copies in Soviet times have been erased from memory, while discussions continue about the extent to which one or other author was complicit with the regime and its demands, or whether an author subservient to the regime's ideology could write a good book. Such attempts to reflect on the past can develop into a critical discourse that moves away from a concern with ideological positions or attitudes and instead deals with poetics, using aesthetic criteria. One of the clear signs of the recovery of literature and criticism is the fact that there are fewer references to politics in literature or in discussions about literature. It seems that, in part, the depoliticization of Lithuanian literature is a reaction to its earlier forced politicization, and while contemporary writing may still deal with political issues, it does so analytically, without the same uncritical acceptance of ideological stances as was the case in earlier writing.

Yet on the path towards independence, Lithuanian literature found itself on the margins. There had been an unspoken expectation that many good literary works would be instantly written or would emerge from drawers where they had thus far been hidden. But such works were very scarce and, in general, no books of significance appeared for several years. This was not because writers were frightened by independence, but because the processes of public life turned out to be much more interesting and more important than literary creativity. The most prominent writers threw themselves into the whirl of public and political life – they took part in rallies, were elected to parliament and fought passionately for independence in the pages of newspapers. Writers became tribunes while literature was set aside for a quieter time.

Now, eighteen years after independence, this is history, albeit recent history which actively shapes the literature of today. Of the writers who made their début under the banner of independence, many grew up in Soviet times and return to this experience in their work; for most writers of the older generation, the past is a major influence in their creative work. It is very likely that these historical changes will remain at the centre of Lithuanian literature for a while, if not directly as a subject, then at least as a formative experience.

THE BIG CHANGES

In order to understand contemporary Lithuanian writing, we must inevitably turn to history. As mentioned earlier, during the years of the Second World War the majority of writers – about 70% – left for the West, spending several years in Displaced Persons camps in Germany before settling overseas, mostly in the USA. For several decades, therefore, the main literary discoveries, marked by this deep trauma, were made across the Atlantic. Works by émigré writers were banned in Lithuania but they still reached Lithuanian readers through illegal channels. Today we call émigré poets such as Antanas Mackus, Alfonsas Nyka-Niliūnas and Henrikas Radauskas poets of international standing, but the writers then in exile felt like strangers. Many lived within the Lithuanian émigré communities, hoping soon to return to their homeland. They didn't therefore attempt to – and, in part, were not able to – join the culture of the host country. That is why today these authors are almost unknown to foreign readers although their impact on Lithuanian literature was immense. After the restoration of independence, many were re-published in their home country, where their work attracted exceptional attention, and eventually helped to paint a more complete picture of Lithuanian literature.

In addition to the return of émigré literature, another important process took place during the first years of independence. Works by Siberian exiles and prisoners were published and numerous memoirs about exile appeared. Readers were also able to discover literature written in the forests and hideouts during the period of the post-war resistance. Not many people in the West will be aware of the fact that resistance against the Soviet occupation in Lithuania was especially strong and went on until 1953 when the last Lithuanian freedom fighter was shot.

One of the interesting phenomena of the last decade has been the success of the essay. The genre thrived against the background of topical publicist writing and memoirs, and gradually penetrated literature and literary criticism. This is probably related to the rapid growth of a subjective approach to writing which had been stifled by the Soviet regime for many years. At the same time, there may be another reason: the borders between genres in modern culture are becoming increasingly blurred with authors writing texts that combine elements of fiction with philosophy and socio-political concerns. The most prominent essayists are not journalists but writers: S. Parulskis, V. Juknaitė, D. Kajokas, H. Kunčius, G. Radvilavičiūtė, the literary historian R. Tamošaitis, the theologian G. Beresnevičius, and the art historian A. Andriuškevičius. Sometimes the divide between literature and the essay is quite elusive. One of the characteristics of the post-modernisation of Lithuanian literature is a dissatisfaction with the limitations of genre which has resulted in attempts to erase the boundaries between literary fiction and non-fiction. A growing number of journals and diaries are being published, with cultural periodicals giving more space to essayistic writing, and this has proved to be so popular with readers that at one time it seemed that non-fiction would overshadow the novel and the short story.

Lithuania is often called a country of poets, even if in recent years this term has acquired a somewhat ironic tone. Indeed, for a long time, poetry played a special role in Lithuania, that of a quasi-religion which offered readers more than other art forms. Poetry was seen as having the potential to preserve the nation, the language and, ultimately, the truth. Even though poetry was restricted by censorship and ideological coercion in Soviet times, it managed to create a uniquely free territory. The liberation of poetry commenced during the period of the Brezhnev thaw, while major poetic developments took shape in the 1970s and 1980s. The official artistic policy of the Soviet system was socialist realism, yet poetry perfected a modernist aesthetic which played a key role in resistance – the poetry of the absurd, polyphonic games with metaphors and blank verse, the use of allusion and writing without punctuation are all examples of such forms of artistic resistance. Frequently, these poetic quests were condemned and the authors banned, but poetry continued to open up more and more to key concerns and to develop the possibilities of poetic language. Thus, after the restoration of independence, poetry was the one genre that continued building on the discoveries of previous decades.

LIVING CLASSICS

Currently, several distinct tendencies in poetry are apparent, the origins of which can be traced back to the 1950s and 1960s. VYTAUTAS P. BLOŽĖ (b. 1930) remains one of the most prominent modernisers of poetic language. In applying surrealist aesthetics, notions of the grotesque and complex rhythms, he creates polyphonies in which reality and imagination merge into a single poetic image. Metonymic links in his poetry reveal unexpected relationships between personal experience and history which, in his writing, acquires a poetic dimension. Thus, he creates an original myth which encompasses universal and personal experiences. In resorting to mythological transformations, he paints an intense image of the world. He is, beyond doubt, one of the most influential Lithuanian poets whose work has had an impact on the younger generations.

Next to Bložė, NIJOLĖ MILIAUSKAITĖ (1950-2002), his late wife and pupil, deserves to be mentioned. At first following in his footsteps,

Miliauskaitė later chose her own path, focusing on quotidian aesthetics, describing woman's life in minimalist language. Yet her poems are not documentaries; they fuse the metaphysical and the mundane of everyday experiences and uncover the deepest layers of the female world. She became one of the most prominent poets of recent decades.

Another major figure is SIGITAS GEDA (b. 1943), an extremely prolific poet and translator. As a translator, he brought to Lithuanian readers a great number of the world's classics, from *The Song of Songs* to the works of Wisława Szymborska and Czesław Miłosz. He is probably the most elemental Lithuanian poet of the twentieth century and his work is permeated with a pantheistic energy which links natural elements with the rudiments of world cultures. In his poetry we can feel the beginnings of poetic language at its very birth. An archaic, pagan view of the world bursts forth in the form of modern poetry and creates the impression that a poem is not written but writes itself. With his considerable influence on the work of younger poets, Geda is often seen as the "shaman" of Lithuanian poetry.

TOMAS VENCLOVA (b. 1937) is the most intellectual figure in Lithuanian poetry. He calls himself a Neo-classicist but he actually writes complex poetry in which Classical forms are filled with existential, historical and political concerns. Often his poems require commentary, and the author offers it during his readings. His poetics are closer to the Russian tradition as we know it from the work of Joseph Brodsky, who was his friend for many years. In 1977, Venclova left for the West as a political dissident and settled in the USA, becoming the best-known Lithuanian poet abroad and one with a profound influence on the younger generation at home. Along with Czesław Miłosz, Vizma Belševica, Knuts Skujenieks, Zbigniew Herbert and Joseph Brodsky, he belongs the poetic generation whose work reflects the importance of political and moral engagement.

Folkloric and ethnographic traditions have, for a long time, played an important role in Lithuanian poetry. The most outstanding representative of this school is MARCELIJUS MARTINAITIS (b. 1936). He subtly combines the poetics of folklore with irony and modern speech. Martinaitis consolidated his position in poetry with the poetic character Kukutis, who is both naive and brimming with popular wisdom. For several decades Kukutis was an Aesopian symbol. It is interesting that Martinaitis' hero appeared in the 1960s, at more or less the same time as Zbygniew Herbert's Mr Cogito. Both Kukutis and Cogito play similar roles: each pretends to be a fool while speaking wisely about the paradoxes and absurdities of life. But Kukutis is a folklore personage, emerging from the archaic experiences of the Lithuanian nation, while Mister Cogito is more of an intellectual, a rational observer. This difference is not accidental: in essence, it draws a line between major trends in Lithuanian and Polish poetry.

Another distinct school is poetry directed at the language itself. The most outstanding representatives of this direction in the 1970s and 1980s were JUSTINAS MARCINKEVIČIUS (b. 1930) and JONAS JUŠKAITIS (b. 1933). Marcinkevičius' poetry, based on love and respect for the Lithuanian language, became a symbol of the resistance to occupation and he is probably the only poet who even today is called a national poet. Juškaitis (b. 1933) is one of the most complex poets in terms of poetic language and form, a creator of multilayered metaphors.

VLADAS BRAZIŪNAS (b. 1952), a member of a later generation, effectively develops poetics based on the linguistic layers of the Lithuanian language, including its various dialects. One should bear in mind that, in the second half of the twentieth century, linguistic experiments and formalist games were not encouraged in poetry, probably because the Lithuanian language had a status than was different from that of other countries. It was a symbol of national resistance and survival, and was thus held in great reverence. It seems that this regard continues to some extent in the work of the younger poets; although the youngest ones no longer shun experimental games and present a more liberal attitude toward the language.

As in many other nations, lyrical existential poetry is alive in Lithuania. Several proponents of this trend are JONAS STRIELKŪNAS (b. 1939), ANTANAS A. JONYNAS (b. 1953) and, to a certain extent, RIMVYDAS STANKEVIČIUS (b. 1973), one of the brightest poets of the younger generation. This poetry consciously chooses Classical landmarks and then refreshes and modernises them.

Several other contemporary poets should not be overlooked. JUDITA VAIČIŪNAITĖ (1937–2001), the brightest creator of urban poetry, painted the world (primarily the female world) in an impressionist style. She was the first to embed urban *realiae* into Lithuanian poetry, with its prevailing agrarian mentality. The poetry of DONALDAS KAJOKAS (b. 1953) is unique because it is informed by metaphysics and oriental poetics, ancient Japanese and Chinese poetry and the philosophies of Buddhism and Shintoism. KORNELIJUS PLATELIS (b. 1951) is dubbed the Lithuanian Ezra Pound. In his work, unlike anyone else, he merges Classical and modern themes, makes use of archetypal and mythical proto-images and creates an ironic picture of the present.

SIX POETS OF THE SIXTIES

When speaking of the generation of poets who were born after 1960 and who made their début in the years of independence, we should emphasise that the renewal of poetry mentioned earlier is more evident in their work. Poets no longer feels they are the "spokesmen of the nation" but on the contrary, that they have to find a language that is in keeping with an increased sense of loneliness and detachment. Poetry becomes more subjective and ironic, an expression of an "I" rather than a "we". The distance between poetry and history, the past and tradition grows and is revised critically. In a post-modern manner, the anxiety associated with the inability to say something original and worthwhile, or the ability to create a personal style, often stimulates an ironic play with the work of colleagues or predecessors – paraphrasing, imitating or mocking. Poetry opens the door to eroticism, "low" language and slang, all of which had, for a long time, been considered taboo or simply not worthy of poetry. Increasingly, narrative is found in poetry, metaphors are avoided and replaced by metonymy; the myths of poetry and the poet are being deconstructed.

* * *

When I was given the opportunity to compile an anthology of recent Lithuanian poetry in English, I decided to present poets of this – my own – generation. The six poets included here grew up in the Soviet era and mostly produced their début collections after independence, having experienced both a lack of freedom and the chance to be free in their creative work. All have a place on the Lithuanian and international literary scene and three have been honoured with the highest award, the National Lithuanian prize. More importantly, however, the group – myself included – forms a distinct literary community, a circle of friends who, in the dreary Brezhnev years, used to meet at private readings and, although we may no longer read to one another, there is a sense that we still write for each other.

AIDAS MARČĖNAS (b. 1960) is one of the most subtle and talented masters of poetic form and counts himself among followers of tradition. Yet in his work he actually destroys the towers of elitist culture. He is ironic about well-established notions of "beauty." He creates a "new naiveté" by resorting to forms of everyday language, paraphrases and other poets' styles. This is, however, a feigned naiveté. The theme of poet as medium, as genius, which he has been developing in his work for a while, is gradually being displaced by an ironic examination of the poet. In the work of Aidas Marčėnas, creating poetry is a key task which becomes evermore difficult to achieve. What remains is poetry about the impossibility of poetry. Marčėnas subtly defines his *ars poetica* in his collection *Eilinė* (Lines), which crowns his work of twenty years. In the epilogue he writes, "We can truly call the process of writing poetry *soulsurfing*, riding the wave of the soul. You really feel certain vibrations and exactly at the right time, not too early, nor too late, you catch the breaking, energy-liberating wave. This requires intuition and skill. And, of course, the will to wade into that stormy iciness. And, clearly, it requires imagination, because without it the ocean doesn't exist. It's true that waves break when they reach the sandbank where a surfer keeps watch. The sandbank is like the life of a poet. That's the meaning of it."

SIGITAS PARULSKIS (b. 1965) is another figure who has made a difference to the development of contemporary Lithuanian poetry. With what he calls "the aesthetics of ugliness" he makes the reader see the world from a different angle – "from below." In his poetry, as in the Carnival described by Bakhtin, the world is turned upside-down, and the reference points are "what is low." Rotting and malodorous objects are in the focus of his poetic vision; a trail of slime, blood and slurry runs through his poems. There is no naivety; it is more like a poetic cruelty which rejects the sweet patterns of existence, searching and longing for holiness and looking for it not in Apollo's heaven but on Dionysus' Earth. Unlike any other Lithuanian writer, the lines of Parulskis' imagination are distorted and magnetised by a strong gravitational centre: death. We can speak of death in a multitude of ways, even without mentioning it. For Parulskis, death becomes the key to his poetics. He mentions it often, and through it he tries to unlock doors; but not to the other, posthumous world, as would be the case with a metaphysically-oriented imagination, but to this world. Through death he tries to feel the shapes of life. Every movement of his imagination "from point A to point B" turns into a journey from life to death, or from death to life. In the past several years, Parulskis has decidedly turned to prose. He writes mostly essays, drama and has published two novels, one of which – *Trys sekundės dangaus* (Three Seconds of Heaven) – met with high acclaim. He no longer writes much poetry, though several new poems are included in this anthology.

GINTARAS GRAJAUSKAS (b. 1966) is a poet and rock musician from Klaipėda, whose position can be defined by his own term "the new intimacy." And indeed, in his work we no longer find the traditional lyrical intimacy and the poetry of sentimental love. Grajauskas rejects "high" metaphorical language, speaks plainly, adopting a narrative principle close to prose, though not associative. Although he views the world with suspicion, at quite a distance, and through the spectacles of irony, he does not end in nihilism or cynicism. What remains in his poems is what is usually overlooked when assessing post-modernist literature: the search for new ways of expression corresponding to changing relations with values, with manifestations of sacrality. There is a longing hidden under the mask of irony. Grajauskas' poetics have already attracted followers, and we can identify a Grajauskas school in Klaipėda. The young poets Rimantas Kmita and Mindaugas Valiukas are among his followers. It is a trend that also dominates contemporary Polish poetry. There are many similarities between Grajauskas and the Polish poet Marcin Świetlicki, who is also a poet and a rock musician. At present, Polish poetry is attracting considerable attention in Lithuania and has seen numerous translations. It can be said that it has quite an influence on Lithuanian poets, especially on the younger generation. In the last few years Grajauskas has tested his pen in other genres – he has published a novel and has written a number of plays that have captured the interest of several theatres.

KĘSTUTIS NAVAKAS (b. 1964) differs from the poets discussed here primarily in that his relationship with the world is determined by aesthetics, which doesn't mean that he is concerned with the beauty of the world, but rather with the aesthetic quality of creative work. For him the world doesn't exist until one of its aspects comes into existence through a poetic or essayistic phrase. Navakas does not seek to create an ontological or structural model of the world; he creates a unique puzzle of details, beneath which we can surmise the hidden concerns of humanity throughout millennia. What he writes about is not visible to the naked eye, it is re-created by the poet as he navigates the surfaces beyond which others cannot see. Characteristically, one of his collections is entitled *Žaidimas gražiais paviršiais* (Playing on Beautiful Surfaces). Navakas is undoubtedly a poet of metaphor, through which he approaches traditional imagery. He builds a home for poetry that is at once cosy and playful, and that shuns banality while being also a space for everyday living. The drama that can be distilled from daily life is especially evident in his most recent poetry book *Atspėtos fleitos* (Imagined Flutes), full of elegance, playfulness and restrained melancholy.

The poetry of DAIVA ČEPAUSKAITĖ (b. 1967) draws on traditional poetics; she usually writes in rhyme and relies on metaphor. Her themes are also traditional: love, call to creativity, and longing for God. Her style, however, is contemporary; it sparkles with postmodern irony, paradox and directs metaphor not at the lofty "heavenly" worlds, but at the everyday, seen from a woman's point of view. And it is here that Čepauskaitė subtly, through seemingly unimportant details, evokes the "unbearable lightness of being", where the desire to be heard, to be loved, meets with indifference and ignorance. It seems that her experience as an actress – she has worked in theatre since 1990 – imbues her poetry with dynamism and a sense of drama. Some of the poems included in this anthology come from her most recent book, *nereikia tikriausiai būtina* (unnecessary surely necessary, 2005), which is mainly written in free verse with a strong narrative element.

My own work belongs to the post-modernist strand of contemporary Lithuanian poetry, but rather than attempt to comment upon it myself, I would prefer to leave that task to fellow writers and critics. I therefore conclude this short essay with a selection of citations which I hope serve to set my poetry within the context of Lithuanian literature today.

"The poetry of Eugenijus Ališanka, while it avoids manufactured hysteria, the draw of nervous language, the destruction of drastic imagery and a particular search for shock value, galvanizes modern form by breaking with traditional grammar at the same time as maintaining a sense of calm within the work... it speaks to those who, through trust in the power of the word and emptiness, open new associative horizons." (Jurga Perminaitė)

"I think that Eugenijus Ališanka has found a manner of speaking, an originally playful intonation which, even when talking of ordinary things, reveals their relationship. Complicated and altogether untangled." (Donaldas Kajokas)

"Eugenijus Ališanka, the representative of high post-modernism who is able to speak without "overripe" metaphors, has created an auto-ironic "eugeniad" in his most recent collections. The lyric subject of his poems is a dynamically self-assessing Eugenijus Ališanka, who calmly documents his life in Vilnius or his travels through a wide geographic expanse, as though he is photographing present-day realities." (Gitana Notrimaitė)

Eugenijus Ališanka

AIDAS MARČĖNAS

PHOTO: VIOLETA ŽALYTE

AIDAS MARČĖNAS (b. 1960 in Kaunas) is a poet, literary
critic and essayist. He studied at the Lithuanian State
Conservatories in both Vilnius and Klaipėda. He has been
a member of the Lithuanian Writers' Union from 1993.
He has contributed digests of periodical literature to
Literatūra ir menas and *Šiaurės atėnai* and has writ-
ten reviews of poetry for the literary journal *Metai*.

His debut collection of poetry, *The Water Well*, won
the Zigmas Gėlė prize for the best first collection of 1988.
His 1993 collection of poems, *Dust*, earned him the lau-
reate's award at the 1994 "Spring of Poetry" festival.
He won the J. Lindė-Dobilas prize in 1999, and received
the prestigious National Laureate's Award in 2005.

Marčėnas's poetry has been translated into Russian,
Latvian, Polish, English, German, French, Swedish and
other languages.

He currently resides in Vilnius.

DĖDĖ

filosofuodamas apie gyvenimą
rašo visokius niekus,
viską nori paaiškinti – kad jau
ligi galo, jei pradeda, tai *ab ovo*,
spyglį mėgindamas apibūdinti
papasakos apie florą
paleozojuje, šiurpindamas
garbius kolegas moralistus
literatūrinio sekso nuotykiais

o po karo užsidirbdavo
dainuodamas vaistinėj, susitaupęs
pats nusipirko vištą, turėjo

kas dieną be žodžių turėjo
personalinį savo kiaušinį

TILTELIS

krūmai, brūzgynai, kur lapę mačiau
ankstų pavasarį, tąkart
šiek tiek nusigandęs galvoju –
pasiutusi gal, jei šitaip arti prisileidžia,
o subtili siela! linkusi savižudybėn

jei kartą pradėjai, anksčiau ar vėliau
padarysi, pavyks – pažinojau
tokią neramią, suicidinę, nepatenkintą
savimi, einančią negrabiai per gyvenimus,
vitališką ir talentingą, nebrandžią

tūkstančius metų, nepatogiai
įsitaisiusią liguistai save mylinčiam
gležno jaunuolio kūne – netikęs
ir šitas nusileidimas, grubus, nepadėjo
durnynas, psichoanalizė, lapė

MY UNCLE

philosophizing about life
he writes all sorts of nonsense,
wants to explain everything – to
the very end if he begins this *ab ovo,*
wanting to characterize a thorn
he will talk about flora
in the Paleozoic era, horrifying
his esteemed moralist colleagues
with literary sexual adventures

and after the war he made a living
in the pharmacy, singing, saving up
he bought a chicken, each day

without words had his
own personal egg

Translated by Jonas Zdanys

THE BRIDGE

bushes, thickets where I saw the fox
in an early spring, at that time
somewhat afraid I thought
maybe it's rabid if it lets me come so close,
o subtle soul! disposed to suicide

once you've made a start, sooner or later
you will finish it, will succeed – I knew
a soul like that, troubled, suicidal, dissatisfied
with itself, walking clumsily through lives,
vital and talented, not maturing

for thousands of years, settling
uncomfortably into the flabby body of an unhealthily
self-absorbed youth – this descent
is worthless, coarse, not helped
by the madhouse, psychoanalysis, the fox

pažliugusiam kovo sniege
pėdsakus andai palikus – sudie, tau sudie ligi kito
krūmokšnio, kur vaizdžiai
į brėkštantį rytą iš samanų prasišviečia
pirmų voveruškų tiltelis

PAKALBĖKIME APIE KERŠTĄ

jei jau toks idiotiškas
paprotys – numirti

mirsiu staiga – kad net
susivokti nespėtų, krutėsiu
krutėsiu ir tik – kaip tai,
dar vakar mačiau, pilnas
buvo sumanymų, kas
pagalvoti galėjo, arba –
nesąmonė, juk buvome
susitarę, taip taip

arba ne – mirsiu ilgai
ir skausmingai, kad matytų,
bjaurybės, kas laukia

that recently left its tracks
in the wet March snow – good-bye, good-bye to you until
the next shrub, where from among the mosses
toward the break of dawn vividly shines
the first chanterelle bridge

Translated by Jonas Zdanys

LET'S TALK ABOUT REVENGE

if it's already an idiotic
custom to die

I'll die suddenly – so they
don't have time to understand, I'll quiver
quiver and only – how can it be
I saw him yesterday, he was full
of plans, who
would have thought, or –
that's ridiculous, we had
agreed, yes yes

or not – I'll die slowly
and painfully, so they'd see,
the bastards, what's waiting for them

Translated by Jonas Zdanys

ARS POETICA

Pasaulis baigias, todėl
reikia rašyti eilėraščius.

Kas dieną tvirtai pasiryžus,
lyg dirbtum kokį prasmingą,
tik tau vienam suprantamą darbą:
statytum namus, laivą
nykstančiai savo šeimynai,
arba restauruotum šventyklą
numirusios andai religijos.

Reikia rašyti eilėraščius
net ir sekmadieniais, nes
tai yra šventė, tai yra darbas,
prilygstantis kunigo darbui.
Nes pasaulis baigias diena po dienos,
pasaulis baigias netgi sekmadieniais.

Todėl reikia rašyti eilėraščius,
reikia statyti namus, jei juose
ir nebus kam gyventi,
reikia kantriai pamatą ręsti
diena po dienos, nes galas,
jei Dievas numirs anksčiau nei kalba,
ir kalba anksčiau nei pasaulis.

TARPTAUTINIS FORUMAS

iš pažiūros protingi, pagyvenę
žmonės, o ką
jie gyvenime veikia? rašo
eilėraščius

tiesiog – rašo eilėraščius

o jei ir veikia
naudingą ką nors,

ARS POETICA

The world is ending, therefore
you must write poems.

Everyday, firmly resolved,
as though doing meaningful work,
work you alone understand,
work like building a house, or
a boat for your dwindling family,
or restoring a holy temple
for a long-dead religion.

You must write poems
even on Sundays, because
Sunday is a holiday and because your work
is like the work of a priest.
And, because the world is ending day after day,
and can end, even on a Sunday.

Therefore, you must write poems,
must build your house, even if
there won't be anyone to live in it
you must patiently lay the foundations
day after day because it is the end
if God dies before language
and language dies before the world.

Translated by Laima Vincė

AN INTERNATIONAL FORUM

intelligent, mature
people, and what
do they do with themselves?
they write poems

they just write poems

and if they do anything
useful

tai vien tam kad galėtų
rašyti eilėraščius

tiesiog – rašyti
eilėraščius, Viešpatie,
kaip gražu

aukštybėse tavo

idiotizmo

GRYNOJO PROTO KRITIKA

protas, vienatinis toks,
nepakartojamas,
nepataisomai šypsantis protas

protingiausias dažniau vakarais
mano grynas mažutis protelis,
jei taip pagalvotum –
turiu ten kažką

protą, vėjo malūną,
protą malantį vėją,
kai išeinu

išeinu pasivaikščiot su šuneliu,
su šikančiu šuneliu
neprotingas,
susimąstęs po žvaigždėmis

they do it simply so that
they may go on writing poems

just writing
poems, Lord,
how beautiful

in the heights

of your idiocy

Translated by Laima Vincė

CRITIQUE OF PURE REASON

the mind, it's singular,
one of a kind,
an eternally grinning mind

it is usually sharpest in the evenings
my pure little mind
if you think of it like that –
I have something there

my mind, a windmill,
a mind generating wind
when I go out

I go out to walk my little dog
with my shitting little dog
I am an idiot
meditating under the stars

Translated by Laima Vincė

DURYS MEILEI IŠEITI

durys meilei išeiti, mylėti
yra tokios mažos durelės

į sodą apleistą

vartai,
prašymais nurašinėti, varteliai

į dangų bilsnoti
melžiamai mirties baimei

nustebusiomis, visada jaunomis akimis
toks plyšiukas

langas mano senatvei
stebėtis viskuo, kas dar juda

langas su pelargonija

Į ALBIONĄ
Unei

Tik noriu pasakyt, kad pasiilgau.
Kad myliu nuolat, erzinuos retokai.
Prisimenu. Bandau įžvelgti šviesą,
kaip savyje – ir retsykiais pavyksta.
Du veidrodžiai viens kitą atspindėjo.
Mes iš tiesų beprotiškai panašūs.

Turėtumei nujausti, kaip keblu man,
kokia graži, kokia miela tu būtum,
save jaunoj mergaitėj atpažinti.
Įsivaizduoju, kad ir tau nelengva,
jei pastebi šį mūsų panašumą.
Ir komiška prašyti atleidimo.

THE DOORS THROUGH WHICH LOVE LEAVES

the doors through which love leaves, the doors
to love are so small,

the doors to the overgrown orchard,

the gates,
covered in scrawled prayers, little gates

knocking at the gilded gates of heaven,
milking the fear of death

with surprised, eternally young eyes –
a little peep hole

a window to gaze out of in my old age,
to watch everything that is still moving,

a window with a pelargonium

Translated by Laima Vincė

TO ALBION
for Une

I just wanted to say that I miss you.
That I love you always, that I'm rarely upset.
I remember. I try to see the light as though it were
inside of me – and sometimes I succeed.
Two mirrors that are reflected back onto each other.
We really are incredibly alike.

You must realize how hard it is for me,
however beautiful, however lovely you might be,
to recognize you in a young girl,
well, I imagine it's not easy for you either,
if you too see how similar we are.
And it's comical to beg your forgiveness.

Bet ką čia aš dabar. Tatanis mirė
prie Franko Zappos biusto. Pangus gyvas.
Nusenęs, smirda iš nasrų, bet mielas.
Sakyčiau – teroristas. Kartais mėgsta
paženklinti Valstijų ambasadą.
Tetukė vis dar kruta, Dievas mato.

Net nežinau, kas „Gustavą" prisuko.
Mamanė veik išmoko slėpti skausmą
po šypsena. Jau sugeba įgelti.
Mama, girdėjau, tartum susilaužė,
nepamenu, gal koją, o gal ranką.
Artūras vėl kažką susižalojo.

O Donį tą, kuris „per amžius skirtas",
atrodo, užvakar mačiau miestely
su apvaloka iš TV projekto.
Tad *om tat sat*, pasaulis nesustoja.
Kaip Robertas, sakykime, pirmasis?
Kas naujo tavo Anglijoje? Anglai?

PRAGARO STALČIUS

stalčiaus pragaras, kuriame
kenčia seni užrašai, nesudeginti
tekstai, rankraščiai, kurie,
kaip žinia, nedega, meilės laiškai

didelės meilės, arba „būtų labai malonu,
kad pasiieškotum prieglobsčio
ir, susirinkęs daiktus, išsikraustytum", kenčia

už visas tavo nuodėmes, šūdžiau

But what can I say. Tatan died
beside Frank Zappa's Memorial. Pangus is alive.
He's grown old, he stinks, but he's sweet.
I'd say, a terrorist. Sometimes he likes
to mark his territory at the US Embassy.
Auntie still gets around, God willing.

I don't even know who winds the clock now.
Nana has almost learned to hide her pain
beneath a smile. She knows how to sting.
Mama, I heard, has broken,
I can't remember, I think, her leg, or maybe her arm.
Artūras has hurt something again.

And Donis, remember the one who "was forever,"
well, I saw him the day before yesterday
in town with a hot woman from a TV show.
Therefore *om tat sat,* the world doesn't stop.
How is Robert, let's say, the first?
What's new in England? The English?

Translated by Laima Vincė

HELL'S DRAWER

in the drawer's hell, where
old notes suffer, unburned
texts, manuscripts, that
as we all know, don't burn, love letters

from a great love, or, letters like "it would be a good thing
if you found a place to go, collected your things,
and moved out," suffer

for all your sins, you shit

Translated by Laima Vincė

TIKRAS EILĖRAŠTIS

pritrėškiau uodą, prisipampusį
mano kraujo – ištryško gyvybė,
kad netgi pagailo šiek tiek, nes
jau niekad, Ardžūna, juk niekad

niekaip nesukurčiau nieko
tikresnio net ir už šitą
kruviną dėmę, šitą
eilėraštį, šitą
siurbusį kraują
lavoną

VIS DAUGIAU ATRABOTKĖS

ir iš tikro kadaise buvau,
kaip ir daugelis mūsų, kentauras,
menamas

motociklas ir menamas
motociklininkas viename, gan lengvai
užsivesdavau

gazuodavau apsiputojęs,
raudavau staigiai iš vietos, tikriausiai
laimingas

tikriausiai keistai turėjau atrodyt
lakstydamas kaip pasiutęs
kalvomis Sapieginės

burzgiantis, atsilikęs nuo bendraamžių,
su savimi
lenktyniaujantis, vienas

maloningasis Viešpats pasakė:
bet juk ir dabar iš tikrųjų niekas
nepasikeitę

A REAL POEM

I squashed a mosquito, bloated
with my blood – its life gushed out,
so that even I felt sorry, because
never, Arjuna, after all, never

never could I create anything
more real than this
bloody mark, this
poem, this blood-sucking
cadaver

Translated by Laima Vincė

MORE AND MORE USED MOTOR OIL

and in fact I once was,
like many of us were, a centaur,
imaginary

by my motorcycle, imagined
as a motorcyclist, I'd start
easily

hit the gas, thrilled,
fly suddenly from my spot, most likely
happy,

most likely I looked strange
flying around madly
over the hills of Sapieginė Park

droning, left behind by my peers,
racing
with myself, the propitious Lord

alone has said:
but now in fact nothing
has changed

ta pati kibirkštis ir tos pačios
trys tave persmelkę gunos,
stūmokliai, tas pats

neišmanymas mechanizmų

PLUNGĖS CENTRINĖS
– visi esame kalti dėl visko, už visus,
visiems ir aš daugiau negu kiti –
turbūt Dostojevskis
Raimondui Jonučiui

tanki ir graži buvo
vasara, debesys
vertikalūs, klausimus

mąslios filosofės reflektavau,
ataidėjau vis labiau
išmintį, gyvenimo

prasmę, senatvę artėjančią
mirtį nesisekė
formuluoti

vasarą visą – jei jau buvai,
jei gyvenai, tai vien tam,
kad išdrįstum

paprašyt atleidimo štai stoviu
Centrinėse kapinėse
svetimoj žemėj

brūkšny tarp mirties ir gimimo
datų nežinia ko
šypsausi

that same spark and those same
three piercing *gunas*,
the pistons, the same

ignorance of mechanisms

Translated by Laima Vincė

PLUNGĖ'S CENTRAL

we are really guilty of everything, for everyone,
towards everyone, and I more than others
probably Dostoyevski
                Raimondas Jonutis

summer was dense
and gorgeous, clouds
rose vertical, I reflected

on the questions raised
by the ruminative philosopher,
I echoed wisdom back ever more,

life's meaning, encroaching
old age, death
I failed to formulate

the entire summer – if you'd already been,
if you'd already lived, then only for that,
to dare

to ask forgiveness and so I stand
in the cemetery
of a foreign land,

in the hyphen between the date
of death and birth, I don't know why
I smile,

nežinia ko prie tavo saulėto
kapo, bičiuli, šypsausi
ir nejaučiu nieko

nieko, vien gumulą
gerklėje, tartum žemėmis
būčiau paspringęs

gumulu tuo, iš kurio –
juk žinai – kartais
išsprogsta poezija

TAI, KAS ĮSIRĖŽĖ
– keli pasiūlymai Rojaus projektui –

prie krepšinio aikštelės, kurios
nebėra, įstrižai augantis
gluosnis, kurio nebėra

į kurį mes, kurių nebėra, vėl ir vėl
mėginam įsibėgėję užbėgti
kaip galim aukščiau

ir šiltose vasaros sutemose
šikšnosparniams
smingant

į dangun metamą akmenuką
kviečiantys grįžt akmeniniai
balsai mūsų motinų

šviesą sugėrę, įkaitę
veik permatomos baltumos
akmenukai, juos mėgom

I don't know why, my friend,
beside your sunny grave, I smile
and don't feel anything,

anything, only a lump
in my throat, as though
I'd choked on the earth,

a lump out of which,
you know, after all, sometimes
springs poetry

Translated by Laima Vincė

WHAT STAYS WITH YOU
A few suggestions for the Paradise project

besides the basketball courts, which
no longer exist, a willow growing sideways,
which no longer exists

that, we, who no longer exist, would try
to run up, again and again, picking up speed,
getting as high as we could

in the warm summer twilight
with bats diving
after stones

thrown up into the sky,
returning to the beckoning voices
of our mothers, still tossing

stones, against the sun
white, see-through,
the kind we liked

krapštyti iš sienos
to blokinio namo krantinėje,
saulėtas špatas

NYKŠTUKINIS

tereikėjo aptikti paukštį
negyvą, nykštuką,
kad tuoj išryškėtų forma

trumpo ir nereikšmingo
nykštukinio eilėraštuko
sergančiam tėvui,

kurį vaikystėje
pravardžiuodavome
mamutu. Siaubingi,

paslaptingi dalykai,
apie kuriuos nesinori
galvoti, protu sunkiai

suvokiami dėsniai vitališko
kūrybingumo, tikrasis
poezijos veidas, tas pats

ironiškai besišypsantis
veidas
poezijos, meilės, mirties

to pick out of the walls
of the concrete apartment block
on the riverbank,
spar

Translated by Laima Vincė

KINGLETISH

all it took was to find a bird,
dead, a kinglet,
to bring alive a form

for a short, insignificant,
kinglet-size poem
for my ailing father,

whom as children
we called the mammoth.
Terrible

mysterious things,
things you don't even want
to think about, things difficult

to understand rationally, lay down
the rules of vital creativity, that true
face of poetry, that same

face, smiling
sarcastically –
of poetry, of love, of death

Translated by Laima Vincė

KĘSTUTIS NAVAKAS

PHOTO: ZENONAS BALTRUSIS

KĘSTUTIS NAVAKAS (b. 1964 in Šeiminiškės, Utenos region) is a poet, essayist, literary critic and translator. He served as chairperson of the Kaunas Young Writers' Section in 1987-1988 and, since 1993, has been a member of the Lithuanian Writers' Union.

From 1994 to 1996 Navakas was culture columnist and literary critic for the newspapers *Kauno diena* and *Noriu*, and worked for Lithuanian State Television from 1998 to 1999 reviewing new books. He owned and ran a bookstore, Seven Solitudes, from 1996 until 2000 and, from 2002 to 2004, worked at Lithuanian State Television on the programme 'Culture House'. He currently writes for the weekly publication *Šiaurės Atėnai*.

Navakas made his literary debut in 1988 with a collection of poetry *Krintantis turi sparnus* (A Falling One Has Wings). He has also published three other books of poetry, a collection of essays, and a collection of humorous literature.

Navakas received the National Award of Culture and Arts and the Julijonas Lindė-Dobilas Prize in 2006. He has translated the poetry of Walther von der Vogelweide, Else Lasker-Schuler, Ernst Jandl, Edgar Allan Poe, Lord Byron, Aloysius Betrand and others. His translations also include several plays and libretti.

Navakas's poetry has been translated into English, German, Swedish, Russian, Georgian and other languages. He resides and works in Kaunas.

SMĖLIO LAIKRODIS
(prisiminimas apie tuos, kurie gyveno veltui)

(neprašyk manęs kalbėti apie smėlį) mes
rinkome kriaukles ieškodami tuštumos
mes dėžes atidarėm

: iš nieno ir iš nieko
iš nebaroko negotikos

iš vėjo ir vėjo (pilno aitvarų bei
liūdnumo) turėjome rinktis
iš properšų ir properšų (neprašyki manęs!)

ar žinai kad štai šitas gvenimas – tavo?

(žiūrėki mirusius neša į žydo namus
ar jauti kaip sekundė tave sutaupo? bet
kur save dėsi) mes

gėrėm žodynų degtinę ir pagirios
būdavo sunkios kol
skyrė mums tylą

kol vedės mus vieną iš kito

(į atmintį medžių) kol stiklo narve
paskutinė smiltelė pakibo

THE SAND CLOCK
(a memory of those who lived in vain)

(don't ask me to talk about sand) we
gathered shells searching for emptiness
we opened boxes

: from nothing and from nothing
from notbaroque notgothic

from wind and wind (full of kites and
sadness) we had to choose
from rifts and rifts (don't ask me!)

do you realize that this is life – yours?

(look they are carrying the dead to the Jewish home
do you feel how a second saves you? but
where will you go) we

drank dictionary whisky and hangovers
were hard until
they assigned us silence

until they led us one from the other

(to the memory of trees) until the last grain of sand
hung in the cage of glass

Tranlsated by Jonas Zdanys

IŠ NEŽINOMO POETO DIENORAŠČIO

PIRMADIENIS

lyg matyčiau dumsias dėmes miegamajam kur kadais gulėjo mano žaislai. aplink juos jau tada saulė spalvą išėdė. iš ko statyti savo pilis bei mėsmales? iš kokio sutirpusio cukraus? tie laikai lyg sukniubę. nuo vėliavų svorio.

pamanykit – vėliavos: tik siūlas ir vėjas. lengvos. jie sukniubo nuo to ką jos reiškė. reikšmė visad gniuždo. su metais pavargsti ir tuomet žaislai galėtų padėti. skardinis šuo ir laivai iš degtukų dėžučių.

aplink tave šitiek saulės. ties jos kraštu ir tavasis kontūras blunka. girdi šnarant? tai senų laikų vėliavos bando tau perduoti skurdų šešėlį. jo ieškai?

nebandai atsisukti. rašai:

tos dvi alkūnės vėl lyg kažkokie stereo-
sargai: kaip nejauku tveriant naują
pasaulį: vis tiek jį užskliaus manojo ribos
: mano triumfas ribosis su mano gėda

ar savo gėdos gėdysiuosi? ne
nes ir paukščius už lango būsiu
teisingai pamatęs / daiktai mano
tekste atpažins vieni kitus / susibus

sakinius ten lyg mažom žirklutėm
iškarpiau: atspėjęs jų slaptą formą
: labai gražu – tačiau ko aš ieškau?

naršau / traukiu iš savęs stalčių po stalčiaus
: jei tai būtų žmogus – pamatęs atpažinčiau
jis turėtų ne mano akis išlestas mano paukščių

ANTRADIENIS

aš pilnas stalčių kiekviename po tetą ar pusbrolį. po kaimynę su vazonėliu klykiančių krokų. geriau gyvenčiau ant bėgių ir per mane važiuotų nepažįstami.

jie prisisegę gražių ženkliukų su kėkštais ir vandens malūnais. lyg išvirkščioji megztinio akis į mane jie žiūri. jei jie būtų stiklas kas vakarą

FROM AN UNKNOWN POET'S DIARY

MONDAY

it's as if I saw smoky stains in the bedroom where my toys once lay. the sun had already eaten away the colour around them. what to build one's castles from but a mincing machine? from what kind of dissolved sugar? those times are as if on their knees. from the weight of flags.

imagine – flags: only thread and wind. light. they fell to their knees under the weight of what they meant. meaning always presses us down. you grow tired with the years and it's then that toys could help. the tin dog and boats made from matchboxes.

around you so much sun. near its edge even your contour fades. do you hear the rustling? it's the flags of the old days trying to hand over a ragged shadow. are you looking for it?

you do not try to turn around. you write:

those two elbows again like some sort of stereo-
guards: how unpleasant creating a new
world: it will still be bracketed by my boundaries
: my triumph will border my shame

will I be ashamed of my shame? no
because I will have correctly seen
the birds outside the window / things in my
text will recognize one another / will wake

sentences then as if I had cut them out
with tiny scissors: guessing their secret form
: it's very beautiful – so what am I searching for?

I rummage / pull out of myself drawer after drawer
: if it was a person – seeing him I would know him
he would not have my eyes pecked out by birds

TUESDAY

I am full of drawers in each one an aunt or a cousin. a female neighbour with a vase of screaming crocuses. it would be better if I lived on the tracks and unfamiliar people rode over me.

they have pinned beautiful symbols with jays and watermills on themselves. they stare at me like a sweater's inverted eye. if they

rinkčiau jų šukes.
nejuntamai. negirdimai. taip visą dieną manyje jie dūžta.
turbūt myliu juos. iš kur man tą sužinoti. aš bijau – jie alsuoja į
mano plaukus. jie kalba.
nebandau išgirsti. rašau:

kartais galvoju: jie trukdo
jie per arti – kaip drabužių siūlės
jie netrunka priminti esantys: tada
einame kur nors į gatves ir parkus

tie mano žmonės su kuriais man
lemta gyventi – jie ima mane lyg
raktus nuo stalo: manimi jie
užsirakina tačiau ant staktos –

vien tik jų ūgis: jų! mano čia
viso ko visur kur prislapstyta ir
nieko viešo (be gatvių ir parkų)

kartais galvoju: trukdau jiems – jie man
viską atvėrė aš suslėpiau net juos pačius
jie mano lobiai aš vienintelis jų piratas

TREČIADIENIS

visada žinau iš kur išeinu tačiau niekad – kur. gyvenu trijų sekundžių
praeitim jos ir užtenka. visa mano dvasia lyg šis žiogo šuolis.
yra dar tūkstančiai metų. apie juos skaičiau spalvotuos moterų
žurnaluos. išsyk pamiršau man užtenka trijų sekundžių. ko nespėsiu
per jas jau niekada nebespėsiu.
išeinu nes ant palangės guli vinys ir plaktukas. po trijų sekundžių
prikals man rankas ir kojas. tuomet spalvotuos moterų žurnaluos
tūkstančius metų grakščiai besisukdamas krisčiau.
mieste turiu savo kelius kurių kelkraščiuos stovi mašinos. jei staiga
pajudėtų išsivežtų mane į daugybę pusių. taip kartais galvą užvertus į
šalis bėga miškas.
jis turi man žinią. nenoriu išgirsti. rašau:

were glass each evening I would gather their shards.

    imperceptibly. inaudibly. that's how they break inside me all day long.

    perhaps I love them. how can I find that out. I'm afraid – they breathe heavily into my hair. they talk.

    I try not to hear them. I write:

sometimes I think: they interfere
they are too close – like the seams of clothes
they don't stop reminding you they exist: then
we go out into the streets and parks

they are my people with whom
I am destined to live – they take me like keys
from the table: in me they
unlock themselves but on the doorjamb –

only their height: theirs! mine here
everything everywhere hidden away and
nothing public (without the streets and parks)

sometimes I think: I bother them – they opened everything
for me I hid even them away
they are my treasures I their only pirate

WEDNESDAY

    I always know where I'm leaving from but never where I'm going to. I live three seconds past her and it's enough. my entire soul like a grasshopper's leap.

    there are still thousands of years. I read about them in women's glossy magazines. I forgot at once that the three seconds were enough for me. what I can't manage in them I never will.

    I go out because on the windowsill lie nails and a hammer. in three seconds they will nail my hands and feet. then in women's glossy magazines gracefully turning for thousands of years I'll fall.

    in the city I have my streets lined with parked cars. if they moved suddenly they would take me in many directions. that's how sometimes, with its head tilted back, the forest runs.

    it has news for me. I don't want to hear it. I write:

kiekvieną kartą užsukęs jaučiuos lyg
čia ir gyvenau – šioj kavinėj
: čia šitaip smagiai prirūkyta pribūta
kiekviename čia keli krislai manęs

rodos visi yra – net dramblių bei
arkliukų norėdamas rastum – juos juk
nešasi visos karuselės (pipirų ant peilio
galo – sako knyga) bet saiko man visad stigo

čia smagu praleisti man atlikusį nereikalingą
laiką (nereikalingą laiką?) ir su metais
reikalingo nebeliks: tačiau kavinėj

šitaip talentingai prirūkyta ir pribūta
kad kas trečia sekundė mane saugo: sukasi
ratu lyg ant dramblių (arkliukų)

KETVIRTADIENIS

 jie visi apvalūs lyg išristi iš trimitų burnų. tik niekas nenuspaudė
ventilių ir jų balsai tušti. nesunkiai galėčiau ką nors pats į juos įdainuoti.
 darbininkai neša suolus lyg neštų didelius sausainius. ir lyja. lietus
liausis bet aš tebebūsiu pasuktas veidu į minią. tai ne mano minia tai
ne mano veidas tai ne mano lietus lyja man į puslapius.
 mes įkalti į tą minią lyg plieno skeveldros. dažnai matau kaip nuo
mūsų jai skauda. ji pratus kentėti ji sėdi mums tarp puslapių ji atėjo
mūsų klastoti.
 kažkas dar gelbsti: stringantys mikrofonai scenarijaus klaidos lietus.
 nesidžiaugiu juo nestoviu jame. rašau:

vėl ta šventė: kas nors pagrojęs trimitą nuleis
ir pasikeisdami ilgai skaitys negabūs poetai
: nejauku man čia – lyg valgyčiau sumuštinių
likučius išrinkęs iš tarpudančių

each time I turn in here I feel as if
I live here – in this café
: it is so pleasantly smoke-filled here, cosy
in each person here are several particles of me

it seems everyone is here – even elephants and
ponies could be found if you wanted – they are after all
on every merry-go-round (peppers on the tip
of a knife the book says) but I have always lacked measure

here it's good to pass my remaining unnecessary
time (unnecessary time?) since with the passing years
not even necessary time will remain: but in the café

so skilfully smoke-filled and cosy
every third second protects me: goes round
in a circle as if on an elephant (pony)

THURSDAY

they are all round as if they had rolled from the mouths of trum-
pets. it's just that no one has pressed the valves so their voices are
empty. it wouldn't be hard for me to sing something into them myself.
workers carry benches as if they are large biscuits. and it's rain-
ing. the rain will stop but I will remain facing the crowd. it is not my
crowd it is not my face it is not my rain that's raining into the pages.
we are hammered into that crowd like slivers of steel. I often see
she is in pain because of us. she is used to suffering she sits for us
between the pages she has come to adulterate us.
something still helps: malfunctioning microphones errors in the
scenario rain.
I do not rejoice in it I do not stand in it. I write:

it's that holiday again: having played the trumpet, someone will lower it
and incompetent poets alternating with one another will read for a
long time
: I feel uncomfortable here – as if I were eating the leftovers of
sandwiches
collected from between their teeth

: negabus poetas! dieve – tarsi negraži
mergina neįstengusi tapti vienu tavo
stebuklų: strėlė negalinti skrieti į
taikinį (jeigu jau juo aš viską matuoju)

skaitant pirštas eilute lyg tų poetų lūpom
slysta: lietus lyja ir jiems ir man
slysta: lietus lyja ir jiems ir man

po to švis: diena ir jiems ir man bus tuščia
po to švis: diena ir man bus tuščia ir
jiems: jų pirštai slys mano lūpom

PENKTADIENIS

   diena naktis. viršus apačia. moteris vyras. juodas švarkas balti
marškiniai. o jei: diena diena. viršus viršus. vyras vyras. juodas švarkas
juodi marškiniai? o jei:
   dienos naktys moterys vyrai knygos drabužiai eilutės tarpai tarp jų
tarpai tarp jų ir nebe jų vien tarpai vien eilutės o po to – juodas švarkas
balti marškiniai? o jei:
   kažkas šito klausos. šitą rašo.
   pats ir rašau:

dieną juk viskas sulieta: kontūrai spalvos
žodžiai taip toli nuo savo daiktų: jie
mašinos – jais patogu važinėti po savo
butą: klausimai paprasti o atsakymų kam man

naktis irgi iliuzija: atrodo viskas pasitraukė
lyg nusikirpus vokus šviesu: stalo lempa
užbrėžė naujo pasaulio ribą: čia
dabar tilps visos mano pamėklės

kartais laukiu – ir nieko! tik klaidinantis
lašas iš įsivaizduotos jūros: plėšau
popierių rūkau glostau kiemo akmenis

: an incompetent poet! god – like an ugly
girl not managing to become one of
your miracles: the arrow that cannot hit
its target (if I already measure everything by it)

the finger reading along the line as if with those poets' lips
slides: rain rains for them and for me
slides: rain rains for them and for me

after that it will brighten: the day for them and for me will be empty
after that it will brighten: the day for me will be empty and
for them: their fingers will slide along my lips

Friday

day night. top bottom. woman man. black coat white shirt.
and if: day day. top top. man man. black coat black shirt? and if:
days nights women men books clothes lines spaces between them
spaces between them and not only their spaces their lines and after
that – black coat white shirt. and if:
someone listens to this. writes this.
I also write:

during the day everything merges: contours colours
words so far from the things they describe: they
are cars – it is comfortable to ride around
your own apartment in them: the questions are simple but why do I
need answers

night is also an illusion: it seems as if everything has retreated
it's as light as if you've cut off your eyelids: the table lamp
has drawn the borders of a new world: here
now all of my ghosts will fit

sometimes I wait – but nothing! only a misleading
drop from an imaginary ocean: I tear
the paper smoke caresses the stones of the yard

jie tikri o manęs čia nieks nepaliudys
stalo lempa neatleis tuščio lapo kol
diena: ak! kaip gražiai vėl viską sulies

ŠEŠTADIENIS

andai sėdėjau po artistės balkonu kol naktis ištiško lyg prakirtus
eketę juodasis pienas. jei būčiau nors įsmeigęs ten šakelę toli ją būtų
nusinešus tąsyk įsisukus žemė. giria iš jos jau šlamėtų ir genys dirbtų
savo triukšmingą darbą.
    niekam nebeskambinu o paskutiniai laiškai man grįžo dar nespėjus
pamiršti adresatų. kur jie dabar. kalbėdavausi su savim lioviausi jei
mokėčiau gročiau koki nors mediniu pučiamuoju.
    geriu tiek daug arbatos. kaip kinai. kinai buvo seni. užsimerkę.
kliuksėjo. beveik telkšojo.
    kam man tie kinai. rašau:

turbūt aš nebegražus turbūt nebeverta
šukuotis prieš kiekvieną eilėraštį: jie jau
keistų brūkšnelių pilni (skyrybos nuovargis)
: jie liudija mane pūvant ir byrant

: jambas mane paliko: keistų metaforų
griūtis išduoda suglebusį kūną: aš
vis dar šokčiau su šešiolikmetėm bet
šnypščiamųjų priebalsių pilni mano posmai

: kažkas mane dar skaito: kažkas kvėpuoja
mano miazmom: kažkam tai patinka – keisti
man tie žmonės: nuo puslapio šviesos balti

turbūt jie serga kaip ir aš: balti nuo morfijaus
o gal aš per toli nuo jų (nuo savęs) lyg mirusi
žvaigždė švytėsianti dar keletą vasarų

they are real but no one will witness me here
the table lamp will not forgive the page until
day: oh! how beautifully everything will merge

SATURDAY

the other day I sat under the actress's balcony until night splashed
out like black milk through a hole in the ice. if I had stuck a small
branch in it would have been carried a long way by the earth that had
screwed itself in there. a forest would have rustled from it and a
woodpecker would have done its noisy work.

I don't call anyone and my recent letters have come back to me
before I managed to forget the addressees. where are they now. I
talked with myself stopped if I knew how I would play some sort of
wooden flute.

I drink so much tea. like the Chinese. the Chinese were old. their
eyes were closed. they were almost stagnating.

what do I care about the Chinese. I write:

perhaps I am not handsome perhaps it's not worth
combing my hair before every poem: they are already
full of odd touches (the exhaustion of separation)
: they witness me decaying and crumbling

: the iamb has abandoned me: the avalanche
of peculiar metaphors betrays a flabby body: I
would still dance with sixteen-year-olds
but my stanzas are filled with sibilant consonants

: someone still reads me: someone breathes
my miasmas: someone likes my work – I find such
people strange: white from the light of the page

perhaps they are as sick as I am: white with morphine
or maybe I am too far from them (from myself) like a dead
star still shining for several summers

SEKMADIENIS

turbūt viską išsakau ir rašymui nekas lieka. viską išsėdžiu kavinėse
išplaunu iš kaimynų keptuvių išbarstau su skaldytais riešutais. krintantis
lašas ir tas man žodį išmuša. ir nėra man priebėgos nėra man luobo
girios geniai mano būsto duris suskaldė.
pro jas ir traukia visos armijos bei karavanai. girios voverės visą
rudenį rita savo kankorėžius. tada ateina jisai spragteli pirštais ir viskas
pranyksta. atsisuka butelio kamštis ugnis įšoka į žvakę ir knyga
atsiverčia ten kur apie mus ir rašė.
jis yra irgi aš tik kitas. jis tiek kitas jog nežinau kaip galiu juo būti.
bijau jog subyrės nuo genio beldimo todėl rašau:

šiandien užėjo kolega: tas kur man
kaip iš graviūros (graverio adata jį lig šiol vis taiso)
: kai vaikšto visi jie gražūs / išvėdinti / išeiginiai
: kai ateina jie dažniausiai atsineša klevo sėklų

jie mano kad iš to vis kas augtų // užėjo:
ką tik jisai savo parašė (dabar kurį laiką
vaikščios) atrodo mato jog man laikas buvo
tuščias: laikau tuščią lapą jo klevo sėkloms

graveris ne virš manęs pasilenkęs // sėdim
: jei mūsų pokalbis nebūtų prasidėjęs prieš du
dešimtmečius – apskritai nebeprasidėtų

tik jo klevo sėklos suktųsi tuščiame mano
lape: bet sėdim: jis kalba lyg valgytų (ir mane)
tik prieš rytą stringa graverio adatai paslydus

SEKMADIENIS PLIUS

lyg matyčiau dumsias dėmes miegamajame kur kadaise stačiau
pilis bei mėsmales. lyg vaikystės ežere saulė degintų mano
atspindžio kontūrą. lyg pieštuku taisyčiau klaidas visuos šalikelių
veidrodžiuos:
rašau. ką man veikti.
už lango lietus arbata ataušo o neįjungtas televizorius kažkur

SUNDAY

I probably say everything aloud and nothing is left for my writing. sit everything out in cafés wash it from neighbours' frying pans sprinkle it with chopped nuts. a falling drop that dislodges a word for me. and there is no shelter for me there is no outer layer forest woodpeckers split the door of my lodging.

through it pass all armies and caravans. forest squirrels roll their pine cones all autumn. then he arrives snaps his fingers and everything vanishes. the bottle top unscrews the flame leaps onto the candle

he is also me but different. he is so different that I don't know how I can be him.

I'm afraid that he will crumble from the woodpecker's knocking so I write:

today a colleague dropped by: the one who seems to me
to come from an engraving (the engraver's needle fixes him even now)
: when they walk they are all handsome / freshened up / in party clothes
: when they arrive they usually bring maple seeds

they believe that something will grow from them // dropped by:
he has just written something of his own (now for a while
he'll walk) it seems he can see that my time
is empty: I hold an empty page for his maple seeds

the engraver is not leaning over me // we sit
: if our conversation had not started two decades
ago in all likelihood it would never have started

only his maple seeds would spin on my empty
page: but we sit: he talks as if he's eating (and me)
just before morning he stops as the engraver's needle slips

SUNDAY PLUS

it's as if I saw smoky stains in the bedroom where I once built castles and mincing machines. as if in a childhood lake the sun would burn the contour of my reflection. as if with a pencil I would correct the mistakes in wayside mirrors:

I write. what else should I do.

rain outside the window the tea has cooled and the unplugged television

giliai savyje rodo trisdešimtį savo programų.
o juk taip ir akmenys. veik viską parodė. įjungti jau daugybę metų.
švytintys.

SONETAI

PIRMAS

mes išgalvojom po šalį kiekvienai
šio pasaulio briaunai: kiekvienai
krypčiai mes visus jos kelius išmelavom

kiekvienas su savo gaubliu mes
sėdim *Trapaus punktyro* kavinėj
kur viskas smilksta greičiau nei degtų

mes parašėm po žodį kiekvienai
pauzei: kiekvieną raidę kirčiavom
kol sieliai vis plaukė mūs laikrodžiais

: kol jų ištakose nebeliko ką kirsti

ANTRAS

nieko neįmanoma sudėlioti iš
paukščių: jie nepaklusnūs jie
išsyk išardys tavo sielą

neįmanoma žaisti paukščiais: jei
jie būtų kauliukai – nė karto
nekristų šešetu

gal kas nors yra kada juos
atspėjęs / ar mokęsis jų metai
po metų: gal kas rado jų svorio centrą

: jie lyg akmenys: mūsų jie nesimokys

that's how stones are shown almost everything. plugged in for
many years.
    glowing

SONNETS

FIRST

we invented a country for every
edge of the world: for every
direction we lied about every one of its roads

all of us sit each with our globes
in the *Fragile Dottedline* café
where everything smoulders rather than burns

we wrote a word apiece for every
pause: accented every letter
while in our watches rafts still floated

: until at their source nothing remained to cut

SECOND

it is not possible to compose anything
from birds: they are not submissive they
will untangle your soul in an instant

it is not possible to play birds: if
they were dice made from bone not once
would they roll out a six

perhaps someone at some time had
figured them out / or studying them year
after year perhaps found their centre of gravity

: they are like rocks: they will not learn from us

DEŠIMTAS

rodos tuoj pat išeitum ten kur
miega granitas: ar kur dūmai
tingiai kyla į viršų lyg jūros žolės

rodos išsyk: bet lieki čia pat
toksai pat: kažkas šion pusėn
tave per stipria ranka sviedė

tad sunerki pirštus ir paklusk
nejaukiems inercijos dėsniams: be tavęs
tavo mintys neturėtų pas ką ateiti

: pasiguosk – jos taipogi sensta ir miršta

VIENUOLIKTAS

šis vėjas veikiausiai iš Ispanijos: jis
neša ristūnų ašutus bei burių
skivytus: tolimais pusžaliais valgiais jis

kvepia / jis persmelkia mus / pro
burną mums muša į vidurius jis
tik vedas ir paklaidinti nedrįstų:

ruoškimės: dar trys dienos ir štai
mūs kieme rekonkista: ristūnų tabūnai
karavelių karavanai hidalgai

: tačiau jei iš kapų šitas vėjas

TENTH

it seems you will soon leave for the place where
granite sleeps: or where smoke
rises lazily upwards like sea grasses

it seems immediately: but you remain right here
exactly the same: someone cast you to this side
with too strong an arm

so lock your fingers together and listen
to inertia's uncomfortable laws: without you
your thoughts would have no-one to come to

: console yourself – they too grow old and die

ELEVENTH

this wind is most likely from Spain: it
carries the trotter's horsehair and the sail's
rags: it smells of distant half-ripe

foods / it pierces us / it strikes
through our mouths to our insides it
only leads and does not dare mislead:

let's get ready: three more days and here
in our yard *reconquista*: herds of trotters
caravans of *caravels hidalgos*

: but maybe this wind is from the cemetery

Translated by Jonas Zdanys

SIGITAS PARULSKIS

PHOTO: AURELIJA CEPULINSKAITE-JARA

SIGITAS PARULSKIS (b. 1965 in Obeliai) is a poet, playwright and essayist. He studied Lithuanian language and literature at Vilnius University and currently lectures on Creative Writing at the Philology Faculty of Vilnius University.

His first book, *All That Out of Longing*, was published in 1990. His other work includes several books of poetry, two books of essays, a collection of short stories and two novels. He is also the author of several plays and scripts for theatre.

In 1991, Parulskis won the Zigmas Gėlė Award for the best literary debut of the year and in 1995 his poetry collection *Of the Dead* received the prestigious Jatvingian Award. His play *From the Lives of the Dead* earned him the 1996 Kristoforas Award for the best young artist's theatre play debut and in 2002 the novel *Three Seconds of Heaven* was recognised as best book of the year and given the Lithuanian Writers' Union Prize. In 2004, Parulskis received the National Prize in literature.

Work by Parulskis has been translated into Russian, English, Latvian, Finnish, Polish, Czech, French, German, Greek, Swedish, Italian and other languages.

He lives in Vilnius.

ŠALTIS

su motina
kartu su motina

žengiau į požemius
į rūsį raugtų agurkų

statinėj sudrumstusi vandenį
pelėsiais apėjusį skystį
motina sakė

ale šaltas vanduo
šaltas vanduo sakiau aš

ir iš kur šitoks šaltis
toks šaltis kad atima ranką

gal iš tamsos
iš nakties ar iš žemės

iš žemės

po žeme bus šalčiau

SUBJEKTYVI KRONIKA
Visi jau mirę
Cézar Vallejo

Mirė galvijų šėrikas Julius, jaučiai užbadė, girtas
gyvulys nemėgsta iš gardo pabėgusių žmonių
mirė Daktariūnas, jį vadindavo Debesėliu, nes
kūrendamas krosnis buvo visiškai juodas
mirė Vytautas Norkūnas, gyveno vienas, žiemą
vasarą avėjo guminiais batais
mirė šlubis Liudvikas Trumpa, jaunas nenorėjo eit
į kariuomenę, buvo įsikalęs į kojos sąnarį vinį
mirė Valerka, užsimušė važiuodamas motociklu, dar
matyt kojos pėdsakas ant stulpo

COLD

Mother
with Mother

we went underground
into the cellar for pickles

the water in the barrel was murky
liquid covered with mould
Mother said

Ah, but the water's cold
the water's cold I repeated

and where does this cold come from
so cold my arm loses feeling

maybe from the dark
from night or from the ground

from the ground

beneath the ground it will be even colder

Translated by Laima Vincė

A SUBJECTIVE CHRONICLE
Everyone is dead
Cesar Vallejo

Julius the cattle feeder – dead,
pierced by steers – drunk,
animals don't like people who escape from the pen.
Daktariunas – dead, they called him Little Cloud,
because lighting the stove he'd be covered in soot.
Vytautas Norkunas – dead, he lived alone, winter, summer, he wore
                                                    rubber boots.
Lame Liudvikas Trumpa – dead, he didn't want to get called up, so
                                                    he banged a nail into his foot.
Valerka – dead, killed riding a motorcycle,
you can still see his footprints on the telephone pole.

mirė pusbrolis Vidas, mėgo žvejot, kai jį laidojo
per bulviasodį, ežeru plaukė dvi gulbės
mirė sunkumų kilnotojas Valdas, buvo įpratęs
važinėt krovininiais traukiniais, nukrito po
ratais
mirė draugo sūnus, jis gimė negyvas
mirė Dievo sūnus, jis irgi mirė negyvas
mirė ir tie, kurių nepažinojau, su kuriais nesisveikinau
net neįtariau esant
mirė namai ir šventyklos, mirė sėklos ir vaisiai
knygos ir maldos, mirė užuojauta artimui
ir gailestis sau
mirė – viskas svarbu
mirė – nieko nėra reikšmingo

DANTŲ GENEZĖ

Tėvas kaip Dievas per
lauką atėjo, pakaustykim
žemę, sako, sūnau

Kaustėm pakaustėm kraujas
tekėjo, prakaitą braukėm
pasėjom pupas

Augo išaugo medis
medinis, o ant to medžio
motina sėdi

Skynė nuskynė motiną
tėvas, įkėlė į medį
gražų mane

Kilo pakilo žemė
įpykus, spyrė į sūnų
medį nulaužė

My cousin Vidas – dead, he liked to fish, when they buried him during
        the potato planting two swans swam across the lake.
The weightlifter Valdas – dead, he was in the habit of riding freight
        trains, he fell beneath the wheels.
My friend's son – dead, he was born dead.
God's son – dead, he was born dead.
Then there are the dead whom I never knew,
never greeted or ever even suspected of living,
then there are the homes and holy places – dead, seeds and their
        fruit, also dead,

books, prayers, compassion – dead
and forgiveness for oneself – dead
everything important – dead
nothing remains.

Translated by Laima Vincė

THE GENESIS OF TEETH

Father, like God, comes
through the fields, let's shoe
the earth, Son, he says

We shod and shod,
blood flowed, we wiped sweat
we sowed beans

A tree grew and grew
wooden, Oh and on that tree
sat Mother

Father plucked Mother
from the tree and
lifted me up

The earth rose
angry, it kicked the son
and the tree broke

Tėvas kaip Dievas rėkia
nugriuvęs, motina medį
į vystyklus supa

Ėjo nuėjo motina
tėvas, medį nuvilko
laukais tuščiais

Sėdžiu ant kelmo pasagą
čiulpdamas, dantys man byra
pasėsiu dantis

SIENA

kiekvieną rytą bėgdavau į šalia esančias
kapines, idant
išblaškyčiau pernakt susikaupusias
sapnų nuolaužas ir nemalonų
kvapą, kuris susikaupia burnoje ir
toje kūno vietoje, kur įtariau
slypint sielą

tai keistos kapinės – viename gale
renkasi katalikai, bedieviai, pravoslavai
kitame – vien tik žydai, nors skaitant
antkapių antraštes sunku patikėti
kad jiems Tora buvo svarbiausi gyvenimo
raštai

vieną dieną kapines perskyrė bjauri
betono blokų siena

aš mėgau kapines – mirties baimė
skatina ją pažinti kuo intymiau, o ne
bėgti tolyn
atsiradus sienai ėmiau vengti
lankytis ten

Father like God shouts
the tree has fallen down, Mother
swaddles the tree

Mother went and went away
Father dragged the tree away
through the empty fields

I sit on the horse-shoe stump
my teeth fall out
I'll plant my teeth

Translated by Laima Vincė

THE WALL

every morning I used to run to the adjacent
cemetery in order to
scatter the fragments of dreams
and unpleasant smells that collected overnight,
gathered in my mouth and
in that place in my body where I suspect
the soul lies dormant

it was a strange cemetery – the Catholics,
the godless and the orthodox gathered at one end
at the other – only Jews, though reading
what was inscribed on the headstones it's hard to believe
that for them the Torah was life's most important
book

one day the cemetery was divided by a hideous
concrete block wall

I liked cemeteries – the fear of death
encourages one to get to know it all the more intimately and not
to run away
when the wall appeared I began to avoid
visiting there

nesišnekantys mirusieji baisiau
nei vienas kitą smaugiantys gyvieji

PELYTĖS ATMINIMUI

melsvoje, ne žydroje
vonioje (ją nuomoju kartu su
kitais buto tarakonais ir langu į
Rytus) radau mažą
pilką pelytę, abu buvome išsigandę

ji čia pateko per ventiliacijos
rankovę, aš kaip ir visi kiti
iš keleto chromosomų kombinacijos

tai įvyko antrąją Velykų dieną, iš ryto
ir mintis nuskandinti pelytę
atrodė šventvagiška
prisikėlimo akivaizdoje

į ąsotį įvaręs, išnešiau ją
į lauką, paleidau, lydėjau žvilgsniu
greitai sprūstančią pumpurus sukrovusių
alyvų link
jau nusigręždamas, verdamas duris
per petį
jaučiu iki šiol
kaip sujaudino bundančią žolę
liesas katino šešėlis

the dead that don't speak to each other are more appalling
than the living who strangle one another

Translated by Medeinė Tribinevičius

IN MEMORIAM OF A MOUSE

in a blue, not sky blue
bath (I rented it along with
the apartment's cockroaches and the window facing
East) I found a small
grey mouse, we were both alarmed

she ended up here via the ventilation
flue, and I, like everyone,
from the combination of a few chromosomes

this happened on the second day of Easter, in the morning
and in light of the resurrection
the thought of drowning the mouse
seemed sacrilegious

I chased her into a jug, carried her
outside, released her, followed with my eyes
the quick scampering towards the bud-laden
lilacs
already turning away, closing the door
over my shoulder
even now I feel
how a lean cat's shadow
unnerved the awakening grass

Translated by Medeinė Tribinevičius

KAŽKAS PRATINAS MUDU MATYTI KARTU

Maudėmės, bridai gilyn, geltonas smėlis
tamsiame vandeny
drumsti ryto vyzdžiai
nedrąsūs pirmieji žingsniai, iš šviesos atgal
į sutemas, tarsi priešais mus plytėtų ne amžinybė
tik ežero gelmė
prie išdegusios laužavietės
rengėmės tylėdami, kiekvienas su savo nuogumu
vienas kitas žodžio nuodėgulis, nė vienos kibirkšties
kad pamėlusios lūpos įpūstų ugnies
tavo mergaitiška figūra su ryškėjančiu
nuovargio kontūru geltonų
ryto vyzdžių dugne, drovus
žvilgsnis į šalį, – po šiukšles besiknaisiojantis
valkata, turėtumėm stoti greta ir dalintis
jo neturto akivaizdumu
nuogi ir sušalę, melstelėjusiom lūpom
melsti šiek tiek aistros
mainais į jo gėdą

vakare, prie mazgojamos kojos prilipęs žalias alksnio lapas
nejaučiau jo, visą dieną buvau su juo
susiliejęs, tarsi jis ir aš niekuo
vienas nuo kito nebesiskirtumėm, tarsi kažkas
pratintųsi mudu matyti ir jausti drauge

POETINIAI INTERESAI

Vos nubudęs supratau, kad esu išmestas iš poetinių interesų lauko
vaikštau aplink aukštą įkvėpimo ir idealų sieną
        niekas negirdi mano balso
ten, viduje, aklas Homeras masturbuojasi svajodamas apie kekšę Eleną
Achilas aprauda meilužį Patroklą
šluba, ūsuota, svogūnais trenkianti Sapfo čiulpia pimpalą
        jaunam jūreiviui, o jam išvykus, ima
        iš nevilties tvirkinti pluksnaakes mergaites

SOMETHING ACCUSTOMS US TO SEE TOGETHER

Bathing, you wade deeper, yellow sand
in dark water
clouds morning's pupils
those wary first steps, from the light back

to the darkness, as though it was not eternity that stretched before us
but only the lake's depths
by the burnt-out fire pit
we dressed silently, each with our own nakedness
one or two firebrand words, not one spark
that our blue lips could blow into flame
your girlish figure developing
the contours of weariness in the depths of
the morning's yellow pupils, a shy
glance to the side, a tramp rooting in the rubbish,
we should stand side by side and share
blatantly in his poverty
naked and frozen, with imploring lips
pray for some sort of exchange of desire
for his shame
in the evening, I find a green alder leaf stuck to my washed feet
I didn't feel it, but we were connected all day
as though he and I do not differ
from one another, as though something
accustoms us to see and feel together

Translated by Medeinė Tribinevičius

POETIC INTERESTS

Barely awake, I understand that I've been thrown out of the field of
poetic interests
and am walking around the high wall of inspiration and ideals
no one hears my voice
there, inside, blind Homer masturbates dreaming about that tramp Helen
Achilles mourns his lover Patroclus
a lame, moustached Sappho, stinking of onions, sucks a young
sailor's cock, and when he's sailed, begins
out of hopelessness, to molest feather-eyed girls

siaurose Aleksandrijos gatvelėse Kavafis medžioja transvestitus,
                                                        nesulaukęs
        barbarų atsiduoda pirmam
        pasitaikiusiam asilų varovui
Li Po girtauja su Omaru, nesaikingai vartodami pilnaties šviesą
Edgaras Po nekrofiliškai apsimetinėja mirusiom varnom
Eliotas mėgina savo seniokišką sėklą ištrėkšti į nevaisingą žemę
o Poundas kalėjime bučiuoja šikną žagarų imperatoriui Musoliniui
supratau, kad siaubingai norėčiau daryti tą patį –
        ištvirkauti metaforų glėbyje
        dulkintis su vestalėmis metonimijomis
atsiduočiau netgi homoseksualiems santykiams su palyginimais, nors
niekad nemėgau jų taip, kaip garbino Raineris Maria, austrų
hermafroditas, vyras, rašantis eiles moteriai, kuri gyvena
                jame pačiame, poetas, sugebėjęs
                užkalbėti dantis pačiam Dievui
noriu, bet negaliu, nes manęs neįleidžia, negirdi mano balso
net jei rėkčiau, kad įminiau Šekspyro mįslę, kad žinau, kieno
                vardu prisidengęs Bibliją kūrė Jahvė
esu tik šešėlis, sėdžiu prie Hado vartų kartu su pasipūtėliu Ulisu
ir pasakoju savo nuoskaudas viskam abejingai tėvo šmėklai
kuri kartas nuo karto gūsteli į mane pelenų vėju
                ir šnabžda
sūnau, užuot kalbėjęs nesąmones, įpilk man nors lašą gyvybės
baisiai troškina šitoj
                sušiktoj amžinybės skylėj

ŠLUOTELĖ

Prie ritualinių paslaugų rūmų stovi automobilis
pravirom durim, vyras, galbūt apie keturiasdešimt, su šluotele
rankoje šluoja iš krovininio salono nubyrėjusius
vainikų lapus, eglių spyglius
gėlių žiedlapius, mosuoja energingai, stengdamasis
užgriebti ir tas
atmosferos daleles, kurios prisisunkę paskutinį

in the narrow streets of Alexandria Cavafy hunts transvestites,
not awaiting the

    barbarians he indulges the first
    donkey herder he comes upon
Li Po drinks with Omar, unconscionably using the full moon's light
Edgar Poe necrophilically plays possum
Eliot attempts to scatter his old seed into infertile ground
and Pound, in jail, kisses the ass of the pederast emperor Mussolini
I understood, horrifyingly, that I'd like to do the same –
    fornicate in the embrace of metaphor
      fuck vestal metonyms
I'd even surrender to homosexual relations with comparisons, though
I've never indulged in them in that way, have not adored them like
Rainer Maria, Austrian

hermaphrodite, man, writing lines to the woman who lives
    within him, poet, managing
    to smooth talk God himself
I want to, but I cannot because they won't let me in, don't hear my voice
even if I shout that I've solved Shakespeare's riddle, that I know in
    whose name Jehovah wrote the Bible
I am only a shadow, sitting by the gates of Hades beside that
arrogant Ulysses

telling stories of my grievances to my father's indifferent ghost
who, from time to time, gusts an ash wind at me
    and whispers
son, for the nonsense you talk pour me even a drop of life
this shit hole of eternity
    suffocates terribly

Translated by Medeinė Tribinevičius

THE LITTLE BROOM

By the centre for ritual services stands an automobile
doors open, a man, perhaps about forty, with a little broom
in his hand sweeps away vine leaves,
pine needles, flower petals
fallen from the backs of lorries, waves energetically trying
also to rake away all the
parts of the atmosphere that are full of the smell

sykį pasivažinėjusio
lavono kvapo.

Paskui jis važiuos namo, veš vaikus į zoologijos sodą
arba prisikraus vaisių ir daržovių didmeninėje parduotuvėje
miesto pakraštyje, susidės darbo įrankius, tuščius
į supirktuvę vežamus alaus butelius, o paskui
vėl šlavinės, prasidaręs duris.

Lipau į kalną, galvodamas apie šluotą
ir šiukšles, – juk visuomet egzistuos
ir viena, ir kita, būsime šluota, ir būsime
šiukšlės, net jeigu gyventume nepiktindami
Viešpaties gailestingumo, –
prisiminiau amerikiečio Randallo Jarrelo eilėraštį
patikusį Radauskui:
iš bombonešio bokštelio vandens žarna
išplaunami šaulio likučiai

BIBLIOTEKA
„staiga atsiveria lentynos ir įeina berniukas… "
Kornelijus P.

Sėdėjau bibliotekos skaitykloj, didelėj salėj
Prie milžiniško stalo, visiškai vienas, mano
kaukolės taurė buvo sklidina
šimtą metų išlaikyto informacijos
vyno, svaigau ir atrodė, nuo
to svaigsta netgi ilgi
šešėliai, krentantys nuo kėdžių
atkalčių

Vėliau, jau į pavakarę prie manęs priėjo niekad
anksčiau nematytas vyras juodais drabužiais
pasisakė esąs prekiautojas, truputį greblavo
tarsi jo gerklėje tariant raidę „r" peršoktų mažas sraigtelis

of the last corpse
driven around.

Later he will drive home, take his children to the zoo
or load up with fruit and vegetables at the wholesale store
on the edge of the city, he will put away his work tools, empty
beer bottles to be driven to the bottle buyers, and later
will sweep again, having slightly opened the door.

I climbed up the hill thinking about the broom
and rubbish – you see, both one and the other
will always exist, we will be the broom and we will be
the rubbish, even if you lived without ever incurring
God's mercy –
I remembered a poem by the American Randall Jarrell
that Radauskas liked:
a gunner's remains
washed from the turret with a water hose

Translated by Medeinė Tribinevičius

LIBRARY

"suddenly the shelves opened and a boy came in... "
– Kornelijus P.

I was sitting in the library reading room, the great hall
by a huge table, absolutely alone, my
skull's goblet brimming
with the wine of information aged a hundred years
my head spun from it, as did
the long shadows
falling from the backs
of chairs

Later, in the evening, a man I'd never
seen before, dressed in black, approached me
he said he was a salesman, burring a little,
the "r" sound a jumping cog in his throat

Siūlė pirkti laikrodį, 1908 metų gamybos, pone, sakė
vyras, nesigailėsit
„Solo" kišeniniai paauksuoti laikrodžiai su grandinėle –
pats geriausias
šių metų pasirinkimas, kiekviena jūsų minutė bus aukso
vertės, o ir aš, pone, – tariant
šiuos žodžius vyriškio balse
pasigirdo patetiškos gaidelės, – turėsiu
ką atsiminti, kai
1943 metais mane, pagyvenusį
trijų vaikų tėvą, nuogą, be
jokios kišenėlės
kišeniniam laikrodžiui, varys
į dujų kamerą

TUŠČIA

Mano batai tušti, ėhė, tušti mano batai
matyti balti druskos dryžiai ant įtrūkusios odos

o kelnės, mano kelnės visiškai tuščios
kur vyriškumas, kur žemės trauka, verčianti
klupti prieš moterį
klešnės sukasi neapčiuopiamos kaip
pustomo smėlio kolonos

ir švarkas, ir švarkas visiškai
tuščias, rankovių nuleistos vėliavos
plaka per išverstas kišenes, nieko
ir ten jau visiškai nieko

kaklaraištis kadaruoja ore
o, ne, po velnių, o ne, niekada
neryšėjau kaklaraiščio, man užteko
savųjų minčių, kurios smaugtų

He offered me a watch, made in 1908, Sir, he said
you won't regret it,
"Solo" gilded pocket watches with chain –
the very best
this year's pick, every one of your minutes will be solid
gold, even to me Sir, saying these words the man's voice
took on a pathetic tone – I will have something
to remember
when in 1943, me an aged
father of three, naked, without even
a little pocket
for a pocket watch, they herd me
into the gas chamber

Translated by Medeinė Tribinevičius

EMPTY

My shoes are empty, aha, empty are my shoes
white salt lines visible on cracked leather

and my pants, my pants are totally empty
where is the manliness, where is the gravity, when made to
kneel before a woman
pant legs twist intangible
as drifting columns of sand

and my jacket, and my jacket is totally
empty, the lowered flags of the sleeves
beating against turned-out pockets, nothing
there is already absolutely nothing

my tie hangs in the air
oh, no, damn it, oh no, I never
wore that tie, my own thoughts
were enough to strangle me

ir vis dėlto, ten, kur būta manęs –
tuščia, visiškai tuščia
drabužiai, namai, pinigai
knygos, draugai, – nuo visų
pamažu nusitrina mano pėdsakas

dar matau, dar paskutinį sykį man leista:
kažkas paskubom kemša senus laikraščius
į tuščius mano batus, kad nosys
per šermenis nebūtų subliuškę
senus laikraščius
su mano tuščia atmintim

VOVERAITĖS

Tavo krūtys, kai išeini iš vonios
kambario – jeigu būčiau tikras poetas, sakyčiau –
iš alyvų giraitės – tavo krūtys panašios
į dvi voveraites, tupinčias ant šakos
 rudi maži snukučiai vos pakreipti į šalis
jos žvalgosi iš aukštai, ką naujo pasiūlys šitas pasaulis

jeigu būčiau poetas, sakyčiau, jog aistros liūtys
plūsteli į mano dubens slėnį, kai matau
tas voveraites, žvelgiančias
į mane kaip į viešpatį, bent jau kaip į fauną
na, mažų mažiausiai, kaip į seną ir
raišą satyrą

galingi geismo srautai teka žemyn,
iš smegenų debesų, per plaučių lapiją
per inkstų akmenis, šniokšdami kepenų rėvose
ir tuomet ten, giliausioje
slėnio oloje suveši, sulapoja
tvirtas kamienas, gyvybės skeptras, *axis mundi*
sakyčiau, jeigu būčiau poetas

and still, there, where I should be –
empty, totally empty
clothes, house, money
books, friends – all traces of me
erased bit by bit

I can still see, one more opportunity is allowed me:
someone is hastily stuffing old newspapers
into my empty shoes, so that during the wake
they won't lose their shape
old newspapers
with my empty memory

Translated by Medeinė Tribinevičius

SQUIRRELS

Your breasts, as you leave the bath
room – if I were a real poet I'd say
emerge from the lilac glen – your breasts are like
two squirrels perched on a branch,
small brown snouts just barely turned to the side
they survey from above what new things this world has to offer

if I were a poet I would say that a deluge of desire
flows into the valley of my pelvis, when I see
those squirrels looking
at me as though at a god, or at a faun
no, at the very least at an old and
lame satyr

potent streams of desire flow down
from the clouds of my brain through the foliage of lungs
over kidney stones, murmur in the liver's shoals
and then, thriving in the deepest cave in the valley
a firm rooted trunk
comes into leaf, sceptre of life, *axis mundi*
that's what I would say, if I were a poet

dabar paprasčiausiai tiesiu rankas tavęs link, ir jaukūs
žvėreliai valgo ramiai iš mano
delnų
ir man sustangrėja, tik tiek

instead I simply stretch my hands towards you, and the tame
little animals eat calmly from my
palms
and I stiffen just a little

Translated by Medeinė Tribinevičius

GINTARAS GRAJAUSKAS

PHOTO: NERIJUS JANKAUSKAS

GINTARAS GRAJAUSKAS (b. 1966 in Marijampolė) is a poet, playwright, essayist, novelist, editor. He won the Zigmas Gėlė Award for best first book of poems with *Tatuiruotė* (Tattoo, 1993). Another collection of his, *Kaulinė dūdelė* (Bone Pipe, 1999), won both the Spring of Poetry and Simonaitytė Awards. His works have been translated into English, German, Swedish and Polish among other languages.

In addition to writing, Grajauskas works as editor of *Klaipėda*, a daily newspaper popular in Klaipeda City and the western part of Lithuania. He is responsible for the selection of literary works and promotion of young Lithuanian writers featured in *Klaipėda*'s monthly literary supplement "Gintaro Lašai" (Drops of Amber).

Having studied jazz at the State Conservatoire in Klaipeda, he also sings and plays the bass guitar in the band *Kontrabanda*.

KAIP NUGALĖTI BERSERKĄ

Iš pradžių jį reikia visaip
siutinti, keikti ir tyčiotis,
kol pasirodys putos

tada įduoti į rankas skydą,
pažiūrėt, ar jau kandžioja
kraštą iš pasiutimo

jeigu jau, tai paduoti ir kardą,
tik atsargiai, ir akimoju
pradangint visus priešus

tai berserkas vis kandžios tą skydą,
pradžioj iš pasiutimo, paskui
susimąstęs

tada jau galima jį pasodinti
saulėkaitoj, duoti duonos plutelę,
tegu sau maumoja

bet nemanykit, kad dabar žinot,
kaip nugalėti berserką

kaip tik tokio berserko nugalėti
niekas negali
joks berserkas

> *Berserkas – mitologinis skandinavų karys, pasižymėjęs ypatinga narsa.*
> *Sakoma, jog prieš mūšį iš įsiūčio kandžiodavęs savo skydą.*

DIEVO DAŽNIS YRA 50 HZ

sėdėjo kirpykloj išmuilinta žiauna
klausėsi radijo FM 91, 4 MHz

o mašinėlėn pakliuvo vandens
tai kaip trenkė per ausis 220 V
net seilės sučirškė

HOW TO CONQUER THE BERSERK

at the beginning you have to infuriate him
in every way possible, to rail and mock at him
until he starts to froth at the mouth

then to put a shield in his hands
to see if he instantly bites
and gnashes the edges

if so, then also give him a sword,
only carefully, and in a split-second
make all his enemies disappear

and so the berserk will keep biting the shield,
at the beginning furiously, later
thoughtfully

soon after, you can sit him down
in the sunshine, offer a crust of bread,
let him munch

but don't think you now know
how to defeat a berserk

namely, such a berserk
cannot be defeated
by anybody
not even a berserk

Translated by E. Ališanka and Kerry Shawn Keys

*Berserk – mythological Scandinavian warrior distinguished by extraordi-
nary courage. It is said he used to bite his shield out of fury.*

THE FREQUENCY OF GOD IS 50 HZ

he was sitting in the barber's lathered up to the gills
listening to the radio FM 91, 4 MHz

and some water got into the electric trimmer
so 220 V slammed into his ears
even the spittle got frizzled

paskui dievagojosi, kad girdėjo
aiškių aiškiausiai, nelyg Vatikano
diktorius būtų ištaręs:
„klausėtės Viešpaties balso".

* * *

pasitrankęs po pasaulį, prakutęs
grįžo namo, dovanomis vežinas
naujoj mašinaitėj

tuoj visa plati giminė susėdo už stalo,
ragavo Jack Daniels ta proga, mandagiai
besiraukydami

keliauninkas, perleidęs pora stiklų
pervirš, kalbos pritrūkus, ėmė ir
pasidejavo

vokiečiai tvarkingi, airiai darbštūs,
olandai vaišingi, tik mes vieni, lietuviai,
išvis neturim kuo pasirodyt

tai tėvokas, sugraibęs lazdą, kaip
užsiautė anam per dantis

sakydamas: bet dabar tai ir tu jau
turėsi kuo prieš kitus pasirodyt

later while crossing his heart he swore he had heard
quite clearly, as though announced
by the Vatican broadcaster:

"You have been listening to the voice of the Lord"
Translated by E. Ališanka and Kerry Shawn Keys

* * *

having traipsed about and lined his pockets
he returned home, carrying presents
in a new car

right away the whole clan sat down around the table,
taking the opportunity to try the Jack Daniels, frowning
politely

after the globetrotter killed a few shots too many,
silence prevailed, and suddenly
he began to complain

the Germans are orderly, the Irish industrious,
the Dutch hospitable, only us Lithuanians
have nothing to flaunt

at that, an old geezer grabbed his walking stick,
slugged him across the mouth

saying: but you certainly
will have something to flaunt now
Translated by E. Ališanka and Kerry Shawn Keys

MAŽASIS BUDA

visada taip:
nei iš šio nei iš to
jie ima rėkti

paskui lyg susitaiko su kažkuo

nutyla ir žiūri į skirtingus kampus
ilgai, kol vėl nei iš šio nei iš to
kaip pradės

aš tada imu ir pasakau
kas ant seilės užėjo, bet garsiai:
rytoj bus debesuota
su pragiedruliais!

(jie apstulbsta: sužiūra vienas
į kitą: beprotnamis, sako kažkuris)

o ką aš daugiau galiu, aš,
66-ųjų metų laidos portatyvinis
radijo imtuvėlis.

TOKSAI KOMIKSAS

iš mano gyvenimo
koksai keistas išeitų komiksas

visuose paveikslėliuose
ilgas važiavimas dulkėtu keliu,
neskubrūs akių judesiai,
smilga šalikelėj

visuose paveikslėliuose
vadelės tarp kelių,
virš galvos, baltame
balionėlyje, tekstas: hm hmm,
halala hmm, – ir mandagūs,

THE LITTLE BUDDHA

it's always like this:
without rhyme or reason
they start shouting

then they sort of make peace with something

fall silent and look a long while
into different corners, until again without rhyme or reason
they start up again

and then I blurt out
whatever comes into my head, even louder:
tomorrow will be cloudy,
with bright intervals!

(they're shocked, start looking at
one another, a madhouse, someone says)

but what more can I do, me,
a little portable radio
of the class of '66.

Translated by E. Ališanka and Kerry Shawn Keys

SUCH A COMIC-STRIP

about my life
what a strange comic-strip it would be

in all the pictures
a long drive down a dusty road,
eyes lingering in slow motion,
crabgrass on the roadside

in all the pictures
reins strapping the knees,
overhead, in a small white
balloon, the text: hmm hmmm,
la-di-da hmm – and polite

tačiau orūs linkčiojimai
kelyje sutiktiesiems

visuose paveikslėliuose
botagas už aulo, sunkūs
vokai ir lūpų kampeliai,
masyvūs arklių pasturgaliai

važiuoji ir važiuoji, važiuoji
sau ir važiuoji

iš vieno paveikslėlio
į kitą

KAŽKOKS KAFKA

gyvenu buv. bendrabučio buv. bufete
(pirmas aukštas, balta veranda)
ir turiu daugybę
kaimynų

keturiais gelžbetoniniais aukštais
ant manęs valgo

keturiais gelžbetoniniais aukštais
ant manęs gulasi

keturiais gelžbetoniniais aukštais
ant manęs stumdo baldus

šalimais toks miškelis, tai ten
dar baisiau: kuosų kolonija

valgo, miega, peri vaikus, triedžia
ant visų, tąso žarnigalius,
nudžiautus iš mėsinės – kas per
linksmybės, koks įvykis, kiek
triukšmo, karkimo ir strykčiojimo

though grave nods
to everyone on the way

in all the pictures
whip sheathed in the boot, eyelids
heavy and the corners of the lips,
massive rumps of horses

you drive and drive, drive
and drive as it were

from one picture
to another

Translated by E. Ališanka and Kerry Shawn Keys

SOME KAFKA

I live in the ex-buffet of the ex-hostel
(first floor, white veranda)
and have plenty of
neighbours

with four reinforced concrete floors
they eat above me

with four reinforced concrete floors
they lie in bed above me

with four reinforced concrete floors
they push pieces of furniture around above me

nearby there's a small wood, there it's
even more hellish: a colony of jackdaws,

they eat, sleep, breed children, shit
on everyone, pull around guts
swiped from the butcher's – what
a lot of hell-raising, what a happening, so much
hubbub, hollering and hopping about

tu matai – ir ten besąs kuosa
poetas: sarkastiškai pražiojęs
snapą, visas nenuoširdus,
kuosų kolonijos gėda

pašaipūnas, maištautojas, prisirišęs
už kojos po medžio šaka žemyn
galva – būtų neblogas
bičiulis: gaila, pastipęs.

TAI JIS

tai jis iš tavo arbatos ištraukia citriną
tai jis pagraužia tavajam stalui kojas
tai jis junginėja šviesas, vaikšto ir
                    spragsi pirštais

jis mėčioja iki lubų tavo vaikus
skambina draugams ketvirtą valandą ryto
paskui trenkia į sieną butelį ir
                    myža į kriauklę

jis ateistas iš prigimties, jis dievo bausmė
jis tavo inkvizitorius ir saldusis kerštas
jis miega su tavo moterim ir miega
                    ramiai kaip kūdikis

jis ateina ir išeina kada panorėjęs
jis tyčia nesako tau kelinta valanda
jis juokiasi iš tavęs, juokiasi net
                    susiriesdamas

jis dažo tavo citriną į cukrų ir kramto
žiūri į akis ir sako: „kada nors tave nužudysiu“
žiūri, linguoja
                    tavo galvą ir šiepiasi.

you see – there's a jackdaw there too
a poet: with beak sarcastically open,
totally insincere,
a shame to the colony of jackdaws

a mocker, a rebel, fastened
by the leg to a branch topsy-
turvy – he would make
a good mate: too bad he's as dead as a doorpost.

Translated by E. Ališanka and Kerry Shawn Keys

IT'S HIM

it's him who plucks a lemon out of your tea
it's him who gnaws the legs of your table
it's him who switches the lights off and on, saunters around and
                                  snaps his fingers

he tosses your children up to the ceiling
calls to friends at four in the morning
then flings a bottle against the wall
                          and pisses into the sink

he's an atheist by nature, he's God's punishment
he's your inquisitor and sweet revenge
he sleeps with your woman and sleeps
                       peacefully like a baby

he comes and goes whenever he wants
he deliberately does not tell you what time it is
he laughs at your expense, laughs
                    even doubling up

he dunks your lemon into sugar and chews it
he looks you straight in the eye and says "someday I'll kill you"
looks, nods
             your head and grins.

Translated by E. Ališanka and Kerry Shawn Keys

POEZIJOS SKAITYMAI

tik paklausyk, kaip gražiai skaito:
išraiškingu balsu, intonaciškai teisingai,
iš anksto pasižymėjęs raudonu pieštuku
loginius kirčius: gabus, bjaurybė,
bėginėja kaip pianistas emocijom

(man tai patinka, kai skaito nelyg
teismo pareigūnas – dabar tik poetai
ir teismo pareigūnai taip skaito:
monotoniškai, žinodami esą pasmerkti
leisti laiką niekam nereikalingiems
formalumams)

bet tu tik paklausyk jo: rodos, ir pats
tuoj pravirks nuo gražumo

pats sau ir varpas, ir kunigas,
ir visa bažnyčia

o pačiame kampelyje
tyli bažnyčios pelė:
eilėraštis

NUOŠIRDŽIAI

jei būtumėm iš tiesų nuoširdūs,
tiek daug nekalbėtumėm apie nuoširdumą

apskritai kalbėtumėm mažiau
ar visai tylėtume

jei būtumėm iš tiesų nuoširdūs,
sakytumėm „nenuoširdžiai užjaučiu"

arba „nenuoširdžiausi linkėjimai".
„nenuoširdžiai Jūsų –
                          Grajauskas"

POETRY READINGS

just listen how prettily he reads:
what an expressive voice, in the right intonation,
marking the logical accents with a red pencil
in advance: gifted, a creep,
he keeps running over emotions like a piano player

(I like it when one reads like
a court official – nowadays just poets
and such officials read like this:
droning away in a monotone, knowing they are condemned
to waste time on formalities
necessary to no-one)

but just listen: it seems that he himself
will burst into tears from the beauty of it all

a bell, and a priest,
and a whole church to himself

while in the far corner
there's the silent church mouse:
a poem

Translated by E. Ališanka and Kerry Shawn Keys

SINCERELY

if we were really sincere
we wouldn't talk so much about sincerity

actually we'd talk less
or keep completely silent

if we were really sincere
we'd say "my insincere condolences"

or "my insincere respects".
"insincerely yours –
                              Grajauskas"

apskritai kalbėtume daug mažiau

lakoniškai

neklausinėtumėm: kaip gyveni, kaip sekasi
klaustumėm tiesiai, kaip sekasi mirti?

ir nuoširdžiai atsakytumėm: ačiū, gerai.

* * *

statau barikadą
aplink save

sustumiu spintą, lovą
pargriaunu šaldytuvą

jie atsiunčia derybininką
picų pardavėją

priešintis beprasmiška, sako jis

priešintis beprasmiška, sutinku

jis išeina kaip nugalėtojas
palikęs picą su krabais

ateina paštininkas: štai jums
registruotas laiškas, pasirašykite

pasirašau, abu šypsomės
priešintis beprasmiška, sako laiškas

nesiginčiju, mandagiai sutinku:
nėra nė mažiausios vilties

tada ateina mormonas – ar tu žinai
dieviškąjį planą, klausia mormonas

overall we'd talk much less

laconically

we wouldn't keep asking: how's life, how's it going
we'd get to the point, how's dying

and we'd reply sincerely: thanks, fine
Translated by E. Ališanka and Kerry Shawn Keys

* * *

I'm building a barricade
around myself

I put the cupboard and the bed together
lay the fridge on its side

they send a negotiator
a pizza-boy

it's useless to put up resistance, he says

it's useless to put up resistance, I agree

he leaves as the victor
leaving a pizza with crabmeat

a postman comes: here you are
a registered letter, sign under here please

I sign, we're both smiling
it's useless to put up resistance, the letter says

I don't argue, I politely agree:
there's not even the slightest hope

then a Mormon comes – do you know
God's plan, the Mormon asks

žinau, priešintis beprasmiška,
sakau aš, mormonas numurma laiptais

tobulinu barikadą: plyšius užkamšau
senais laikraščiais ir kramtomąja guma

skambina vėl į duris, ir vėl

už durų picų pardavėjas
mormonas ir paštininkas

ko gi dar, klausiu aš

buvote teisus, sako jie, priešintis
beprasmiška, ir ėra nė mažiausios vilties

todėl esame vienoj
barikadų pusėje

KINESKOPAS

tas daiktas į kurį žiūrime
vadinasi kineskopas

jis tik atrodo plokščias
o iš tikrųjų yra kaip krepšys
pilnas mažų taškelių
šokinėjančių tarsi
švytinčios kalėdinės
blusos

kai taškeliai gauna įsakymą
klusniai stoja į savo vietas
ir susidėlioja į „medį", „dangoraižį"
„Balkanų krizę" ar „L. di Caprio"
(tik pažvelk, kaip šviečia jo „balti
marškiniai" – tai vis nuo taškelių)

I know, it's useless to put up resistance
I say, the Mormon murmurs down the stairs

I improve the barricade: I draft-proof cracks
with old newspapers and chewing gum

they ring at the door again, and again

at the door are the pizza-boy
Mormon and postman

what else I ask

you were right, they say, it's senseless
to put up resistance, there's not even the slightest hope

that's why we're on the same
side of barricade

Translated by E. Ališanka and Kerry Shawn Keys

SCREEN

the thing we are looking at
is called a screen

it just seems to be flat
but actually it's like a basket
full of small dots
jumping about like
glittering Christmas
fleas

when the dots get the command
they obediently take their positions
and get set into "a tree", "a skyscraper"
"a Balkan crisis" or "L. di Caprio"
(just take a look how his "white
shirt" shines – it's because of the dots)

taigi jei pamatysi ką nors
baisaus – nesigąsdink, nesiduok
apgaunamas

nėra ten nei džiunglių, nei potvynių
anei zombių su zeimeriais

bet aš nesakau, kad nieko nėra
(kaip kad sako tamsybininkai)

yra begalinė daugybė

taškelių

KAS YRA INTERNETO CENTRE

mistikai sako:
interneto centre tupi voras

netiesa netupi

sako profiai

taik tik didžiausias
pasaulio šiukšlynas
pilnas benamių
su naršyklėmis

įdomiausia jog internetas
yra Niekur

mes ten turime
savo adresus

so if you see something
monstrous – don't get scared, don't let yourself
be fooled

there are neither jungles nor floods there
nor zombies with chainsaws

but I'm not saying there's nothing
(as obscurantists say)

there is an infinite quantity

of dots

Translated by E. Ališanka and Kerry Shawn Keys

WHAT IS AT THE CENTRE OF THE INTERNET

mystics say:
a spider keeps house at the centre of the internet

not true, no nesting there

say the pros

it's just the biggest
scrap-heap in the world
full of the homeless
with browsers

the most interesting thing is the internet's
Nowhere

right there
our own address

Translated by E. Ališanka and Kerry Shawn Keys

DAIVA ČEPAUSKAITĖ

PHOTO: VLADAS BRAZIUNAS

DAIVA ČEPAUSKAITĖ (b. 1967 in Marijampolė) is a poet and dramatist, and a member of the Lithuanian Theatre Association and the Lithuanian Writers' Union. She graduated from the Kaunas Medical Academy as a physician. She also took acting classes at the Kaunas Youth Musical Studio. Since 1990 she has been employed full-time as an actress by the Kaunas Youth Chamber Theatre.

Čepauskaitė has published three collections of verse and is also known as an author of plays for children. Her dramatic pieces have been staged by Lithuanian theatres. *The Birthday of Pimpė* (1990), *The Cold Heart* (after the fairy tale by Wilhelm Hauff, 1997), and *The Nightingale* (after the fairy tale by Hans Christian Andersen) were staged by the Kaunas Youth Chamber Theatre; while *The Mystery of a Snowball* (1999), *When a Star is Falling* (after the fairy tale by Andersen, 2001), and *The Potato Tale* (2001) were staged by the Kaunas Puppet Theatre.

Her poetry has been translated into English, Swedish, Finnish, Russian, Italian and other languages.

At present, she resides and works in Kaunas.

* * *

Sekmadienis.
Nesiseka.
Tik seka
šlapia katė
akim lakuotom
paskui vėją
savaitgalio bespalvį.
Jokio kvapo –
valerijono nei žuvies,
nei riebalų.
Sakiau, kad nieko gero.
Tik muilo putų
šleikštus aitrumas, žmonės
vaikus mazgoja.
Jauniausiajam iš jų
ant subinės mėlynė,
taip jam ir reikia, nenušveisi,
trink netrynęs,
tokia daili, ir forma – pasagėlės.
Taip jam ir reikia,
todėl kad kvailas
ir jauniausias.
Ir nieko gero
iš jo nebus.
Labai jau meniška mėlynė
ant subinės.

LOPŠINĖ MYLIMAJAM

Durneli, tu mano
durneli,
vienu du gyvi telikome,
visi seniai mirę,
nuprausti, nuskusti,
sušukuoti, nugrimuoti,
apraudoti, palaidoti,
tvarkingai išrikiuoti,
gėlėmis apkaišyti,
ilsisi ramybėje

* * *

Sunday.
Not going well.
Just a wet cat
with lacquered eyes
following
the colourless wind
of the weekend.
Not a smell –
neither valerian nor fish
nor grease.
Nothing good.
Just the nauseous pungency
of soapsuds, people are
washing children.
The youngest one
has a bruise on his behind,
he had it coming, you won't scrub it clean,
try as you might,
what a pretty piece of work – a tiny horseshoe.
Because he's stupid
and the youngest.
And nothing good
will come of him
Too artistic,
the bruise on his behind.

Translated by E. Ališanka and Kerry Shawn Keys

LULLABY FOR A LOVED ONE

You fool, my little
fool,
only the two of us are left,
everyone else is long dead,
washed, shaved,
combed, made up,
mourned, buried,
neatly lined up,
decorated with flowers,
resting in peace

be jokios rizikos.
Vienu du niekaip
negalime numirti,
krentame žemyn galva
vis į tą patį dangų,
vis iki kito karto.
Akių kampučiuose
budi dvi kanarėlės,
skirtingos kaip dvi
vieno žmogaus akys,
durneli, tu mano
durneli,
šiąnakt ir vėl niekaip
negalime numirti,
šiąnakt verkiu kanarėlėmis,
ir mano ašaros čiulba.

KAIP PATEKTI Į ROJŲ

Reikia turėti drąsos
parašyti eilėraštį,
reikia turėti drąsos
nerašyti eilėraščio,
reikia sakyti labas
ir sudie,
reikia gerti vitaminus,
reikia gerbti visus
ir mylėti vieną,
net jei nėra už ką,
reikia tyliai kentėti
ir kantriai tylėti,
reikia tylėti, kai visi kalba,
ir kalbėti, kai visi tyli,
reikia išnešti šiukšles,
palaistyti gėles,
sumokėti už dujas ir vandenį,
už klaidas ir sėkmę,
reikia atiduoti širdį

with no risk.
We alone can find
no way to die,
fall head first
always into that same sky,
always until the next time.
In the corners of our eyes
stand two canaries,
different as two
of the same person's eyes,
you fool, my little
fool,
tonight once again we can find
no way to die,
tonight I weep canaries
and my tears sing.

Translated by Jonas Zdanys

HOW TO GET INTO PARADISE

You need to have courage
to write a poem,
you need to have courage
not to write a poem,
you need to say hello
and goodbye,
you need to take vitamins,
you need to respect everybody
and love just one,
even if he doesn't deserve it,
you need to suffer silently
and patiently keep silent,
you need to be silent, when everybody's speaking,
and to speak, when all keep silent,
you need to take the rubbish out,
to water the flowers,
to pay for gas and water,
for mistakes and successes,
you need to give the heart

už akį ir akį
už dantį,
reikia nereikalauti nieko,
kai norisi visko,
ir reikalauti visko,
kai nieko nesinori,
reikia laiku užmigti
ir laiku nubusti,
surasti du kairiuosius batus,
nes kiti abu dešinieji,
reikia laukti ne tam,
kad grįžtų, ir grįžti
ne todėl, kad laukia,
reikia žiūrėti į dangų,
nes jis į tave niekada
nežiūrės,
reikia numirti, nes reikia,
netgi tada, kai nesi
to vertas,
reikia parašyti eilėraštį
iš baimės,
tarp "taip" ir "ne",
iš "kodėl",
su "kam",
už "ačiū"
netgi tada,
kai nėra už ką

NORIU PASAKYTI

Noriu pasakyti – myliu,
bet gėda,
dar apsijuoksiu,
todėl sakau – nekenčiu.
Noriu pasakyti – nekenčiu,
bet neturiu priešų,
todėl sakau – į sveikatą.
Noriu pasakyti – labas,
bet galiu pasakyti per garsiai,

for the eye, and the eye
for the tooth,
you must not ask for anything
when you wish for everything,
and demand everything,
when you wish for nothing,
you need to fall asleep on time
and to wake up on time,
to find two left shoes
because the other two are right ones,
nor wait for somebody to return,
nor return
because someone is waiting,
you need to look at the sky
because it will never look
at you,
you need to die because you need to,
even when you don't
deserve it,
you need to write a poem
out of the fear
between "yes" and "no",
from "why",
with "what for",
for "thanks",
even when
it's not deserved

Translated by E. Ališanka and Kerry Shawn Keys

I WANT TO SAY

I want to say – I'm in love
but I feel ashamed
of making such a fool of myself,
so I say – I hate.
I want to say – I hate
but I have no enemies,
so I say – cheers.
I want to say – hello
but I might say it too loud,

todėl apsimetu nepastebėjęs.
Noriu pasakyti – sudie,
bet bijau, kad sugrįšiu,
todėl nieko nesakau.
Noriu nieko nesakyti,
bet bus per tylu,
todėl sakau – lyja.
Noriu pasakyti – šalta,
bet gali neišgirsti,
todėl šilčiau apsirengiu.
Noriu pasakyti – eisiu,
bet šalia nieko nėra,
todėl paprasčiausiai einu.
Noriu pasakyti – žvirblis,
bet gal ne taip supras,
todėl sakau – akmuo.
Noriu pasakyti – skauda,
bet jau sakiau,
todėl sukandu dantis.
Noriu pasakyti – smarvė,
bet negražu,
todėl nekvėpuoju.
Noriu pasakyti – velniop,
bet ir taip aišku,
todėl sakau – sriubos nori?
Noriu pasakyti – kodėl,
bet į kvailus klausimus
niekas neatsakinėja,
todėl sakau – nieko, nieko.
Noriu pasakyti – gražu,
bet dėl skonio nesiginčijama,
todėl sakau – vakar.
Noriu pasakyti, bet nesakau,
nes negaliu, o kai galiu – nenoriu.
Noriu pasakyti – noriu,
bet norai ne visada pildosi,
todėl sakau – karamelė
arba šiaip kvailystė.
Noriu pasakyti – taigi,
bet tokiais atvejais nieko nesakoma,

so I pretend I don't see anyone.
I want to say – goodbye
but I'm afraid I'll return
so I say nothing.
I want to say nothing
but it will be too silent,
so I say – it's raining.
I want to say – it's cold
but no one will hear
so I put on warm clothes.
I want to say – I'm going
but there's nobody around,
so I simply go.
I want to say – sparrow
but maybe it'll be misunderstood,
so I say – stone.
I want to say – it hurts
but I've already said it,
so I clench my teeth.
I want to say – it stinks,
but that would be uncouth,
so I hold my breath.
I want to say – to hell
but it's evident without saying it,
so I say – some soup?
I want to say – why
but nobody replies
to stupid questions,
so I say nothing, nothing.
I want to say – it's nice
but nobody argues about taste,
so I say – yesterday.
I want to say but I do not say,
because I can't, and when I can't – I don't want to.
I want to say – I want
but wishes don't always come true,
so I say – caramel
or I say humbug.
I want to say – uh-huh,
but in such cases nothing is being said,

todėl sakau – geras oras.
Noriu pasakyti – be reikalo,
bet be reikalo, šiaip sau
juk nešnekėsi.

* * *

Yra toks žaidimas –
suraski, kas šviečia,
kas šviesiau už tamsą.
Ką radau, tą ir užrašiau:
plieninė durų rankena,
baltas vyno kamštis,
mylimo padai,
varlės pilvas,
sidabrinės balandos,
sidabrinės lapės,
laboratorinės pelės,
vanduo,
nebūtinai švarus,
akys,
nebūtinai stiklinės,
ypatingai šviečia
plaukų segtukai
ir adatos,
šuns liežuvis,
apčiulptas saldainis,
dar šiek tiek ugnis,
plaučių uždegimas
ir motinos pienas,
dar šiek tiek mūsų
pradžia
ir galas,
dar šiek tiek
popieriaus lapas
iki eilėraščio

so I say – the weather's nice.
I want to say – no matter,
but if it's of no matter
you wouldn't speak at all.

Translated by E. Ališanka and Kerry Shawn Keys

* * *

There is a game –
find what shines,
what is brighter than darkness.
What I've found I've written down:
the steel handle of doors,
the wine's white cork,
the soles of my lover,
belly of a frog,
silver goosefoot,
silver foxes,
laboratory mice,
water,
not necessarily clean,
eyes,
not necessarily glassy,
and these are especially shiny:
hairpins
and needles,
the tongue of a dog,
half-sucked candy,
and a bit more: fire,
pneumonia
and mother's milk,
and a bit more: our
beginning
and end,
and a bit more:
a sheet of paper
awaiting the poem

Translated by E. Ališanka and Kerry Shawn Keys

* * *

Šiek tiek saulėlydžio
panagėse,
o gal tik seno kraujo,
šiek tiek prisiminimų
ir maldos šiek tiek,
kad baigtųs vakaras
kaip kregždė,
aukštielninka parkritus
ant dangaus

RAGANA

Tavo mylimoji yra ragana.
Ji sėdi po raudona musmire
ir žiūri į vieną tašką.
Ji įsipjovė pirštą,
kad tau skaudėtų,
apsibintavo galvą,
norėdama nubausti tave,
ji nėra fotogeniška,
kad nuotraukose tu
atrodytum gražiau,
ji tyli ir neatsako į klausimus,
nes yra labai užsiėmusi –
ji myli,
ji renka viską, ką randa gatvėje,
nes galvoja, kad tai tu pametei,
ir nuolatos ką nors pameta,
kad tu surastum,
ji skolinasi viską iš visų,
nes nori gražinti tau,
ji viską pamiršta,
nes nori, kad tu primintum,
ji painioja tavo vardą su kitų,
nes nori, kad dar kartą
pakartotum savąjį,
ji numezgė tau megztinį

* * *

A little bit of sunset
under the nails,
perhaps stale blood,
a reminiscence or two
and a bit of a prayer,
to bring evening
to an end
like a swallow
on its back
in the sky

Translated by E. Ališanka and Kerry Shawn Keys

THE WITCH

Your beloved is a witch.
She sits under a red fly agaric
entranced by one of its spots.
She cut her finger
for you to feel pain,
and bandaged her head
wanting to punish you,
she's not photogenic,
in order for you
to look nicer in photos,
she keeps silent and doesn't answer questions
because she's very busy –
she's in love,
she picks up everything she finds on the street,
because she thinks you've lost it,
and permanently loses something
for you to find it,
she borrows everything from everyone
because she wants to return it to you,
she forgets everything
because she wants you to remember,
she confuses your name with others'
because she wants you to repeat
yours again,
she knitted a sweater for you

su šešiom rankovėm,
kad stipriau apkabintum,
naktimis ji miega,
kad į ją žiūrėtum,
ji yra arti,
nes yra trumparegė,
o kai išeina į tolį,
visada pasiklysta,
tada atsisėda po raudona
musmire ir laukia, kol surasi,
taip ryškiai ir kantriai laukia,
o skruzdėlė keliauja
nuo pado iki smilkinio
ir atgal jau kokį šeštą
kartą.

* * *

Lyg ir pavasaris.
Kiemuos daugiau vaikų,
murzinų delniukų geldelėse
šyla smėlis.
Atbėga upė
ir nubėga.
Joje žuvis,
kurios nesugavai.
Bala nematė,
dar pastovėsiu
su kmyno sėkla tarp dantų.
O dešinėj suoliukas,
kur trys senutės
lyg trapūs sausainiai
subyra nuo pietryčių
vėjo.

with six sleeves,
so you'd embrace her harder,
at night she sleeps
so you can look at her,
she's near
because she's near-sighted,
and when she goes far away
she always gets lost,
then she sits down under a red
fly agaric and waits until you find her,
she waits so pointedly and patiently
that an ant travels
from her foot to her temple
and back
maybe six times.

Tranlsated by E. Ališanka and Kerry Shawn Keys

* * *

It's like Spring.
More children playing in the yards,
the sand getting warmer
in the shells of small dirty palms.
The river comes running
and runs away.
There's a fish in it
which you haven't caught.
Let it ride,
I'll keep standing for a while
with a caraway seed between my teeth.
And on the right there's a bench
where three old ladies
crumble like biscuits
before the southeast
wind.

Tranlsated by E. Ališanka and Kerry Shawn Keys

* * *

Jau laikas gultis,
tik palauk, aš apsirengsiu
visus rūbus, kuriuos turiu,
visus lig vieno,
suknias ir marškinius,
ir kailinius storiausius.
Manęs bus daug,
aš būsiu didelė,
sunki aš būsiu,
galvosi – tai bent moteris,
tiek darbo
turėsi ligi ryto,
kol išlukštensi
spenelį, rusvą, mažą
tarsi kregždės
šūdeliukas.

POEZIJA

Esu karvė, vardu Poezija,
duodu šiek tiek pieno,
paprastai 2,5% riebumo,
kartais pavyksta
išspausti ir iki trijų,
didžiuojuos, kad jis apdirbamas
pažangiausia technologija
ir popieriniuose tetrapakuose
pasiekia nereiklius vartotojus,
sergu visomis ligomis,
kurios nesvetimos gyvai būtybei
ir kruopščiai aprašytos
veterinarijos vadovėliuose,
ganausi geroje bandoje
(kolektyvas draugiškas,
kalbos barjerų nėra),
bijau sparvų ir zootechniko,
galiu būti ir kitaip naudinga –
užėjus šalnoms, kai nusilengvinsiu,

* * *

It's time to go to bed,
just wait, I'll put on
all the clothes I have
down to the last one,
gowns and shirts
and the bulkiest of furs.
There will be a lot of me,
I'll be big,
I'll be heavy,
you'll think – what a woman,
you'll have so much to do
till morning,
before you husk
the nipple, russet, tiny
like a swallow's turd

Translated by E. Ališanka and Kerry Shawn Keys

POETRY

I am a cow named Poetry,
giving some milk,
usually 2.5% fat,
sometimes I manage
to force it up to three,
I am proud that it is processed
by the most advanced technology
and in paper cartons
it reaches undemanding consumers,
I can get sick with any disease
not foreign to living creatures,
and thoroughly described
in veterinarian manuals,
I keep pasturing in a good herd
(the collective is friendly,
there are no language barriers),
I am afraid of gadflies and horse doctors,
I can be useful in other ways as well –
when the early frost comes and I relieve myself,

įlipk į mano krūvą basas,
pamatysi – tokia šiluma,
nuo padų pakils
iki pat pakaušio.

come climb into the dung barefoot,
you'll notice such a cosy heat
rising up from your feet to the very crown
of your head.

Translated by E. Ališanka and Kerry Shawn Keys

EUGENIJUS ALIŠANKA

PHOTO: AUTHOR'S ARCHIVE

Eugenijus Ališanka (b. 1960 in Barnaul, Russia) is a poet, essayist and translator. Following his graduation from Vilnius University with a degree in mathematics, he worked for the Culture and Art Institute of Lithuania and then, from 1994-2002, as a director of international programmes in the Lithuanian Writers' Union and a director of an international poetry festival "Spring of Poetry" (Poezijos pavasaris). Since 2003 he has been working as editor-in-chief of the magazine *Vilnius*, published in English as *The Vilnius Review* and in Russian as *Вильнюс*.

Ališanka is a member of the Lithuanian Writers' Union's Board and of PEN. He has published five books of poetry and two collections of essays. In 1992, *Equinox* (1991) won the Zigmas Gėlė Award. *The Return of Dionysus* (2001) received the Lithuanian Minstry of Culture Award.

Ališanka has translated poetry by Zbigniew Herbert, Wisława Szymborska, Carolyn Forshé, Dannie Abse, Bernardine Evaristo, Jerome Rothenberg, Desmond Egan, Aleš Debeljak, Marcin Świetlicki, Jacek Podsiadło, Michael Schmidt, Pascale Petit, John Freeman and others. He has also received a 'Spring of Poetry' award for translation of poetry.

His work has been translated into English, French, Polish, Swedish, Russian, Finnish, German and other languages.

Ališanka lives and works in Vilnius.

IŠ KAULŲ LIGOS ISTORIJOS

šešis šimtus metų skaudėjo kaulus viduramžiais tampė juos ilgino pagal
gotikinio grožio kanonus renesanso žydėjimo metais kareiviai plakė
jaučio odos rimbais ant gėdos stulpų klasicizmo epochos architektai
taikė auksinio pjūvio taisyklę kažkodėl socializmo laikais vadintą
prokrusto lova pirmojo pasaulinio karo metais tąsė šunys iš vienos
fronto linijos pusės į kitą antrojo metais virė ūkinį muilą pokary
išrengdavo iki nuogumo kiekvieną kauliuką tiek ten kur ir nusišlapinti
šaltyje buvo nelengva tiek ir čia katedros aikštėje dūzgiant musėms
dešimtame dešimtmetyje dar pasirodydavo kaulus traiškančių
mechanizmų nors daugiau suko artritas ir lankstė radikulitas bet kaip
rašo pseudo-eugenijus dutūkstantaisiais metais kaulai išnyksiantys ir
žemė įžengsianti naujajan naujojo dievo be kaulų eonan

ŽIURKĖS

išretėjęs dangus pirštu dursi ir plyšta šviesa
kaulai ir tie išretėję vos išlaiko istoriją
tiesią laikyseną lietų per visą liepą
per visus laikus ta pati karma žiūrėti į dangų
žiurkės akimis pilkųjų kūnelių generacija
miesto archyvuose suslėgtas oras kol išgrauždavo
tunelį iki kito gyvenimo užakdavo akys užtrūkdavo
moterys jokio žaismo vienkryptis eismas iki žiemos
pabaigos iki sniego ant kryžių ant vyrių
ant pilko kūnelio neeuklidinis laikas virtuvė
sovietmečio lempa nedekartiškas protas palikdavo
dar trupinių nebylė šokdavo pilka uodega
per belmonto miškus rokantiškių kalnais
nekabindama mirusių kiek prisimenu nieko nebuvo
kiek užmiršau buvo po virtuve po obuoliniu vynu
po primos pelenais žiurkės ir tiek išgraužė žodyną
ir tiek

FROM THE CASE OF BONES

for six hundred years the bones ached in the middle ages they were
stretched according to the Gothic canons of beauty during the Renais-
sance soldiers whipped them on pillars with lashes of ox-leather in the
era of Classicism the architects put into practice the rule of the golden
section for some reason called the bed of Procrustes in Soviet times
during the First World War dogs dragged them from one front line to
another during the Second World War soap was rendered from them in
postwar times each small bone was stripped there where it was even
difficult to piss in the cold as well as here in Cathedral Square buzzing
with flies in the century's last decade one could see mechanisms crush-
ing bones but more often arthritis and radiculitis bent them but as pseudo-
eugenijus writes in the year two thousand bones will disappear and the
earth will ascend into the new aeon of a new boneless god

Translated by E. Ališanka and Kerry Shawn Keys

THE RATS

threadbare sky thrusting a finger through it the light cracks
even bones there are rarefied barely holding history barely an
upright carriage the rain through july through all ages the same
karma to watch the sky with a rat's eyes this generation of grey
corpuscles stale air in the city's archives while they would gnaw out
the tunnel to the next life rats' eyes overgrown the women
dried up no game one-way traffic to the end
of winter until the snow on crosses on hinges
on the grey corpuscle non-euclidic time the kitchens
the lamp of soviet times the non-cartesian mind a few
crumbs left dumb it used to jump with its grey tail
over the forests of the belmont hills of rokantiskes cemetery
not touching the dead as much as i remember nothing
as much as i forget it was under the kitchen under the apple wine
under ashes of prima rats and only rats gnawing the dictionary only that

Translated by E. Ališanka and Kerry Shawn Keys

prima rats: a type of cigarette

ESĖ APIE LIETUVIŲ LITERATŪRĄ

vis rečiau pajėgiu atsakyti į klausimą kodėl rašau
kartais atrodo: tam kad rašyčiau
kartais matau šviesą
vis mažiau mane domina poezija (juolab proza)
kartais atrodo: skaitau tam kad užmirščiau
kartais atrodo: esu kitapus šio nevalingo žodžių žaismo
vis dažniau prisiverčiu būti tarp lietuvių poetų
kartais jie širdingi ir skausmingi kaip rusų poezija
kartais jie girti ir agresyvūs kaip repas
kartais jie nesantys kaip aš
vis kukliau galvoju apie lietuvių poeziją
kartais prisimenu tik vieną kitą vardą: vytautas alfonsas sigitas
kartais sakau: ji išmokytų meno bet ne gyvenimo
kartais klausiu: argi jai rūpi kaip kokiam celanui gyvenimas
kartais tyliu: toks neišmanymas prisišauks bėdą

GERIAU VYRAI NESURAS

jie smirdi arkliašūdžiais
pavėjui šukuodami plaukus jie
seka paskui prekijų vilkstines

jie smirdi piligrimų nakties
šlapimu supuvusiais vaisiais
dūmais iš skerdžiamo jaučio širdies
šieno pakratu gyžtančiu pienu

jie smirdi česnaku po meilės
nakties stovinčiu vandeniu jie plėšia
atsilikusius sapnus kritusius gyvulius
vieniši būriais vegetarai mėsėdžiai

jie smirdi saldžia rugine
pirmaisiais eilėraščiais apie meilę
vėliau apie mirtį jie smirdi
neprieinama uoslei gyvybe

ESSAY ON LITHUANIAN LITERATURE

less and less am I able to answer the question why I write
sometimes it seems: in order to write
sometimes I see the light
less and less the interest in poetry (not to mention prose)
sometimes it seems: I read in order to forget
sometimes it seems: I am behind this involuntary play of words
more and more I force myself to be with lithuanian poets
sometimes the poets are big-hearted and tortured like in russian poetry
sometimes drunken and aggressive like in rap
sometimes barely there like me
more modestly I think about lithuanian poetry
sometimes I remember only a few names: vytautas alfonsas sigitas
sometimes I say: poetry can teach art not life
sometimes I ask: does life care for poetry like celans
sometimes I am silent: this ignorance will bring trouble upon me
Translated by E. Ališanka and Kerry Shawn Keys

NOTHING BETTER FOR MEN

they stink of horseshit
combing their hair against the wind
they follow caravans of peddlers

they stink of urine of night's
pilgrims of rotten fruit
of smoke from the heart of slaughtered oxen
they stink of straw bedding of milk going sour

they stink of garlic after a night
of love of stagnant water they plunder
the dreams trailing dead animals
they plunder alone in gangs vegetarians carnivores

they stink of sweet rye
of the first poems of love
followed by those of death they stink
of a life inaccessible to smell
Translated by E. Ališanka and Kerry Shawn Keys

KAIP TAVE PAŽINAU

sūrios silkės gimsta sūrioje jūroje
taip galvojau vaikystėje
ir dabar taip manau
tavo kūnas yra sūrus tavo žaislai
tavo žaizdos
druska ant kaulų druska
sniege druska po pagalve
taip galvojau mėnulio druskos kalnai
užtvenkia pieno upes druskos gyslos
įtempia ugnikalnių raumenis druskos
kasyklose meldžiasi druskos dievo totemui
iš druskos
taip manau ir dabar
panašus pažįsta panašų

KLAUSOS ANATOMIJA

visad girdžiu kraujo tvilksėjimą
kažkur po smilkinio dauba
ir su gyvųjų balsais nesutaikomą
spengsmą iš kaukolės centro
užveržtą mazgą galugerkly
rezginį pirmykštės baimės
ir kito gyvenimo nuojautos
virpesį papilvėj nuo brendimo
pradžios tarsi būčiau gyvybę
duodantis ir garbę atimantis žvėris
traukulius pakinkliuos stovėdamas
altajaus kalnuos tarsi dievui
iš dešinės lengvą tirpenimą paduos
kai aptinku eilėrašty
neparašytą eilutę

HOW I KNOW YOU

a salted herring lives in a salty sea
as a child I thought this way
and I think the same way now
your body is salty your toys
your words
salt on bones salt
in snow salt on the pillow
in this way I thought the hills of the moon
were salt damming up rivers of milk
veins of salt stretching muscles of volcanoes
the totem of the salt god
of salt prayed for
in salt mines
I think the same way now too
like knows like

Translated by E. Ališanka and Kerry Shawn Keys

ANATOMY OF HEARING

I always hear the pulsing of blood
somewhere under the notch of the temple
and a tingle from the centre of the cranium
incompatible with the voices of the living
a tightening knot deep in the throat
a tangle of primordial fear
and portent of another life
a quivering above the pelvis since the beginning
of pubescence as if I were a beast
bringing in the same breath life and dishonour
cramps behind the knees while standing
in the altai mountains as if at the right
hand of god a light numbness in the sole
when I come upon an unwritten line
of a poem

Translated by E. Ališanka and Kerry Shawn Keys

EPIKŪRO RUDUO

neturėčiau skųstis, malonumų netrūko, gal mažiau moterų, daugiau filosofijos, bet šiandie neturėčiau gailėtis, su filosofija susilaukiau daugiau vaikų, plika akim atpažįstu, tegu retai matausi, bet šitaip ir gamtoj surėdyta, dabar dažniausiai vienas, kūno ne kaži kiek likę, kokį dūmą per dieną sutraukiu ar taurę stipresnio išlaižau, šiaip vis knygos, vis vienodesnės, ypač odiniais viršeliais, kaip ir moterys, pamenu, jaunystėj kiekviena buvo vienintelė gyvenime, skaitydavau, kol siūlių nebelikdavo, dabar visos kaip tos piemenės olimpo stadione, perkarusios, turinys be formos, niekuo neprisidengusios, gryna fizika, ryškus aristotelio mokyklos kvapelis, jokio malonumo, kadaise rašiau dienoraštį po dienos nuotykių, dabar tik atsiminimus, ką gi, irgi malonumas, pasakoti istorijas, ypač nebūtas, visą gyvenimą melavau sau, dabar galiu ir kitiems, vienintelis belikęs

TURISTINIAM SEZONUI PRASIDĖJUS

mirusieji vaikšto su mažais žemėlapiais
rankose

akivaizdu anam tai pirmoji kelionė
nebuvo išvykęs iš gimtojo kaimo
toliau rajono centro
ir še tau užsienis
tikriausiai europa galvoja
tik mirksi blyksi naktį šviesu kaip dieną
kokio velnio dabar
karvės nemelžtos šienas pūva
kelio klausti nedrįsta
prasčiokų kalba
jau norėtų namo

tas tikrai miręs
ne sykį
ieško reichstago eifelio bokšto
myžančio berniuko iš bronzos
raudonųjų kvartalų

THE AUTUMN OF EPICURUS

I shouldn't complain, there was no lack of pleasures, maybe fewer women, more philosophy, but today I shouldn't regret this, with philosophy I sired more children, they're recognizable to the naked eye, though we seldom meet, but in the natural world it's like that, now I'm mostly alone, not much of the body left, during the day I puff on a few cigs or sip some hooch, otherwise just books, always more and more alike, especially those bound in vellum, like women, I remember when I was young every book was the only one, I used to read them until the stitching frayed and fell apart, now they're all like those nymphets in the olympic stadium, sheer slabs, content without form, not covered with anything, pure physiques, an aristotelian odour, no pleasure, once upon a time I used to write in a diary after the day's adventures, now I just jot down memories, well, it's a pleasure as well, to tell stories, especially cock-and-bull tales, all my life I lied to myself, now I can lie to others as well, it's the only pleasure left.

Translated by E. Ališanka and Kerry Shawn Keys

START OF THE TOURING SEASON

the dead are walking about with small maps
in their hands

for that one it's obviously the first trip
he never went further from his native village
than to the centre of the district
and my stars, a foreign country
probably europe he thinks
winks and blinks at night as bright as day
so where in the hell am I
the cows aren't milked the hay's rotting
he daren't ask the way
in his rough tongue
he'd already like to go home

another one surely
has died quite a few times
he's looking for the reichstag the eiffel tower
the pissing boy made of bronze
the red quarters

žodžiu lankytinų vietų
pažymėtų žvaigždutėm
ne viskas taip kaip turėtų būti
toli gražu ne viskas
bet suka ratus
žiūrėk jau ir devintąjį
šitam nesvarbu
rojus ar pragaras
visus užkampius apeina
pasitikrina žemėlapius

žilų senukų grupė
visi elegantiški
akiniai auksiniais rėmeliais
derančiais prie rojaus ikonografijos
tęsia savo amžinas atostogas
įpročio neatsisakę
papsėti pypkę
seka gidą
daugiau žiūrėdami po kojomis
dažnai fotografuojasi
ir čia jaučias laikini
vis bijo atsilikti

vaikšto mirusieji su mažais
žemėlapiais
ne kiekvienas iškart randa
brandenburgo vartus
su keturiais pragaro žirgais
ar triumfo arką
su karalystės insignijomis
vieni blaškos tarp keturių
raudų sienų
kiti sėdi pergamono bistro
neskubėdami siurbčioja alų

kiekvienas turi savo mažą
žemėlapį

in a word for the must do's
designated with stars
not everything's as it should be
on the contrary everything's
not he's walking in circles
already the ninth
for this one it doesn't matter
whether it's heaven or hell
he explores every last cranny
checking his maps

the group of grey-haired elders
all swank
spectacles with golden frames
befitting the iconography of heaven
continue their eternal vacations
not yet having abandoned the habit
of puffing on a pipe
they follow the guide
being careful not to trip
often taking pictures of themselves
feeling their own transience
constantly afraid of falling behind

the dead follow on with small
maps
not everyone can find at a single blow
the brandenburg gate
with the four horses of hell
or the triumphal arch
with insignias of the kingdom
some of them jerk about
amid four wailing walls
one sits in the bistro pergamum
sipping beer not in a hurry

everyone has his own small
map

Translated by E. Ališanka and Kerry Shawn Keys

CURRICULUM VITAE

gimiau alkanas
baigiau žaidimą klasėmis
diplomuotas melancholikas
visą gyvenimą dirbau padienius darbus
didžiausias stažas – kišenvagio
trumpai dirbęs klapčiuku prie vieno dievo
ir grabdirbiu prie kito
šiuo metu esu sezoninis rašytojas
gyvenu vienas su žmona ir sūnumi
esu išleidęs daugiau knygų negu parašęs
paskelbęs dešimtis paraiškų
apeliacijų ir aplikacijų
kelis pasiaiškinimus
šiemetinis kelių policijai apdovanotas
kultūros ministerijos premija
bėgių maratono laureatas
prašyčiau darbo pagal specialybę
kur nors prie žemės
kad ir piemeniu
su dūdelės alga

SKAITYMO MALONUMAS. BARTHES

tai ne vienintelis gyvenimas
gal vienas iš geresnių
galbūt net įmanomas
nė vieno tikrinio vardo
jokių paso duomenų
nė vienos sąskaitos už moteris
elektrą aukščiausiojo teismo išlaidas
jokių bilietų jokių alibi
kino teatrų salėms paryžiui
perkeltinėms prasmėms
viso labo knyga
apie keturis metų laikus
kurią suskaitau per valandą
gurkšnodamas kavą
kanalo krantinėj per lietų

CURRICULUM VITAE

I was born hungry
graduated from the game of hopscotch
certified melancholic
all my life I've been a day labourer
most prestigious job – a pickpocket
briefly, I worked as an acolyte for one god
and then as a pine-box carpenter for another
at present I do seasonal work as a writer
I live alone with a wife and son
I've launched more books than I've written
issued dozens of requisitions
appeals and communiques
several apologies
this year one to a traffic cop
received a prize from the ministry of culture
I am the laureate of the train marathon
I should request a job to match my speciality
something grounded earthy
maybe a shepherd
with a reed-pipe for my salary

                    Translated by E. Ališanka and Kerry Shawn Keys

THE PLEASURE OF THE TEXT. BARTHES

this isn't the one and only life
though it may be one of the better ones
it might even be possible
no proper names
nor passport data
not a single bill for women
no electric bill high court expenses
no tickets no alibi
for theatre halls for paris
for figures of speech
just a book
about the four seasons of the year
which I read in an hour
sipping coffee
on the quay of the canal in the rain

net neįtariu
kad tai vienintelis gyvenimas
stiklo šukių sauja
kurią suspaudžiu
iki smėlio smilties
galbūt net įmanomas

SCENARIJUS

laikas: amžiaus pradžia
vieta: didmiestis turintis ateitį
pirma scena: kavinė ankstyvą rytą
veikėjai: užsimiegojęs kavinės šeimininkas
ir pirmasis lankytojas
pirmas veiksmas: jaunuolis geria kavą
ir skaito *europos saulėlydį* originalo kalba
susimokėjęs išeina knygą palieka ant stalo
antra scena: ta pati kavinė dieną
veikėjai: žvalus kavinės šeimininkas
ir pietaujantys tarnautojai
antras veiksmas: pietaujantys gyvai
aptarinėja euro kursą varto laikraščius
trečia scena: kavinė vakare
veikėjai: pavargęs kavinės šeimininkas
ir po darbo dienos sugužėję vietiniai
trečias veiksmas: vietiniai geria alų
visu garsu televizorius
transliuoja europos futbolo čempionatą
ketvirtoji scena: kavinė prieš užsidarant
veikėjai: kavinės šeimininkas
ketvirtas veiksmas: šeimininkas skaito
europos saulėlydį
uždanga

I don't even suspect
that this is the one and only life
a fistful of splintered glass
which I squeeze
into a grain of sand
might even be possible

Translated by E. Ališanka and Kerry Shawn Keys

SCRIPT

time: beginning of the century
place: city with a future
first scene: a café early in the morning
characters: groggy owner of the café
and first customer
act one: a young man sipping coffee
while he reads the *the decline of the west* in the original
he pays and departs leaving the book on the table
second scene: the same café later in the day
characters: upbeat owner of the café
and workers having lunch
act two: the diners thumb through newspapers
engage in a lively discussion about the Euro exchange rate
third scene: café at night
characters: tired owner of the café
and locals flocking together after work
act three: locals drinking beer
TV at full blast tuned
to the European football championship
fourth scene: the café before closing
characters: owner of the café
act four: the owner reads
the decline of the west
curtain

Translated by E. Ališanka and Kerry Shawn Keys

FOTOSESIJA

juodas retro kostiumas baltų marškinių
viršutinė saga prasegta
tarsi nuolat trūktų oro
už nugaros bėgiai
tarsi nuolat trūktų stočių
peronuos lūkuriuojančių moterų su gėlėmis
erotinio traukinių ritmo
tinkamo fono statiškai figūrai
žuolių rimo netvarkingam gyvenimui
juodi akiniai apniukusią dieną
kurie pasiteisina prieš objektyvą
fotografas išvengia raudonų akių efekto
net jeigu tik balta ir juoda
net jeigu fotografas tik viešpats
kuriam pozuok nepozavęs
vis tiek sulaukia momento
kai nuima akinius
kai užsega viršutinę marškinių sagą
tada ir suveikia blykstė
juodi blizgantys batai dar nė dulkelės
švarūs kaip sąsiuviniai rugsėjo pirmąją
tarsi po vasaros nežinotum kokia kalba
sugrįžti į save
iš pavykusios nuotraukos

SU SAVAIS

paprastai sekmadienį
renkuos paskutinę eilę
dar geriau stovimos vietos
už kolonos
kur pasiekia tik aidas
niekad tiesioginė kalba
ypač kai rimta
kai skaito pamokslą
ar kviečia vakarienei
geriausia už durų
klausaus tuomet kaip dūzgia bitės

PHOTOSESSION

a black retro suit the upper button
of a white shirt unbuttoned
as if the subject lacks air
an iron railing behind his back
as if some footing were needed
women standing around with flowers on the platforms
erotic rhythm of trains
fitting background for a static figure
rhyme of the crossties for a disorderly life
sunglasses on an overcast day
by countering objectivity
the photographer escapes the red-eye effect
even if only in black and white
when the lord is the photographer
you can pose all that you want
nevertheless the moment arrives
when glasses are taken off
when the button of the shirt is buttoned
precisely when the flash comes into play
black polished shoes without a speck of dust
clean as the exercise books on the first of september
as if after summer you don't know in which language
to return to yourself
from such a tailored photo

                    Translated by E. Ališanka and Kerry Shawn Keys

WITH MY OWN KIND

usually on sunday
I choose the last row
standing-room's even better
behind a column
where only the echo reaches
never the direct speech
especially when it's serious
delivering the sermon
or the invitation to a banquet
it's best outside
then I listen to how the bees hum

nešdamos medų
viešpačiui tiesiai į ausį
pastoviu nenusiėmęs kepurės
tada kišuos pirštus į burną
ir švilpiu kaip moku
subėga maži ir dideli
grynakraujai ir be dokumentų
nusišėrę ir raupsuoti
traukiam šunkeliais
palei tvoras
ieškodami nuotykių
paprastai sekmadienį
esu su savais

carrying honey
straight into god's ear
I stand for a while cap on head
then stick two fingers in my mouth
and whistle as best I can
they come running then small and big ones
pure-blooded without papers
mangy and leprous
we dog down the back roads
along fences
looking for adventures
usually on sunday
I am with my own kind

Translated by E. Ališanka and Kerry Shawn Keys

KERRY SHAWN KEYS' roots are in Appalachia. He lives in Vilnius, where he taught translation theory and creative composition as a Fulbright lecturer at Vilnius University. He has dozens of books to his credit, including translations from Portuguese and Lithuanian, and his own poems rooted in rural America and Europe, and in Brazil and India where he lived for a considerable time. His work ranges from theatre-dance pieces to flamenco songs to meditations on the Tao Te Ching, and is often lyrical with intense ontological concerns. Recently, he has been writing prose *wonderscripts* and monologues for the stage. A children's book, *Land Of People*, won a Lithuanian laureate for artwork he co-authored. He often performs with the free jazz percussionist, Vladimir Tarasov – they released a CD in the Spring of 2006. Recent books are *Conversations With Tertium Quid* and *The Burning Mirror.* Keys received the Robert H. Winner Memorial Award from the Poetry Society of America in 1992, and in 2005 a National Endowment for the Arts Literature Fellowship. He also received the Translation Laureate Award from the Lithuanian Writers' Union in 2003. He was a Fulbright Research grantee for African-Brazilian studies. He is a member of PEN and the Lithuanian Writers' Union. Selected poems have appeared in Czech and Lithuanian.

MEDEINĖ TRIBINEVIČIUS is a Canadian writer and translator of Lithuanian literature. She was born in Orillia, Ontario and grew up on Manitoulin Island. In 2006 she completed an MA in English at the University of Toronto. Her poetry and prose (in English) has been published in *The Walrus*, *Room Magazine*, *Misunderstandings Magazine* and *The Shore*. She is currently finishing a novel. Her translations have been published in the *PEN International Magazine*, *The Vilnius Review*, *Nine New Works of Prose from Lithuania: 2005-2006,* the Druskininkai Poetic Fall almanac and in other publications. Current projects in-

clude co-translating e.e. cummings into Lithuanian with poet Benedik-
tas Januševičius, and translating *Tūla*, a novel by Jurgis Kunčinas,
into English.

LAIMA VINCĖ is a graduate of Co-
lumbia University, School of the
Arts MFA program in Creative
Writing. She is the recipient of a
National Endowment for the Arts
fellowship, two Fulbright lecture-
ships, a PEN Translation grant, and
an Academy of American Poets
award among other honours. Writ-
ing under Laima Sruoginis, she is
the editor and translator of three an-
thologies of contemporary Lithua-
nian literature: *The Earth Remains* (Columbia University Press),
Lithuania In Her Own Words (Tito Alba), and *Raw Amber* (Poetry
Salzburg). She has translated four books of literary nonfiction from
Lithuanian into English. Her novel for children, *The Ghost in Hannah's
Parlour* was translated into Lithuanian and published by Gimtasis
Zodis and was well received in Lithuania. In Autumn 2008, the Lithua-
nian Writers' Union Press will publish in English and Lithuanian *Len-
in's Head on a Platter*, a memoir of her year as a student at Vilnius
University in 1988-1989 during the time of Lithuania's singing revolu-
tion. Laima Vince also writes as a journalist on contemporary social
issues in Lithuania.

JONAS ZDANYS was born
in New Britain, Connecti-
cut, in 1950, a few
months after his parents
arrived in the United
States from a United
Nations camp for Lithu-
anian refugees. He is a
graduate of Yale Univer-
sity and gained a Ph.D.
in English literature from
the State University of
New York. He is the au-

thor of thirty-seven books, thirty-four of them collections of his own
poetry, written in English and in Lithuanian. He has received a number
of prizes and book awards for his own poetry and for his translations

of Lithuanian poetry. He has taught at Yale University and the State University of New York and serves presently as Chief Academic Officer in the Connecticut Department of Higher Education. He lives in North Haven, Connecticut, with his wife and daughters.

Eugenijus Ališanka (b. 1960 in Barnaul, Russia) is a poet, essayist and translator. Since 2003 he has been working as a chief editor of the magazine *Vilnius*, published in English as *The Vilnius Review* and in Russian as *Вильнюс*. He is a member of the Lithuanian Writers' Union's Board and of PEN. He has published five books of poetry and two collections of essays and his work has been translated into English, French, Polish, Swedish, Russian, Finnish, German and other languages. In 1992, *Equinox* (1991) won the Zigmas Gėlė Award. *The Return of Dionysus* (2001) received the Lithuanian Minstry of Culture Award.

Ališanka has translated poetry by Zbigniew Herbert, Wisława Szymborska, Carolyn Forshé, Dannie Abse, Bernardine Evaristo, Jerome Rothenberg, Desmond Egan, Aleš Debeljak, Marcin Świetlicki, Jacek Podsiadło, Michael Schmidt, Pascale Petit, John Freeman and others and has received a 'Spring of Poetry' award for his translation of poetry.

As well as co-translating many of the poems in this book (including his own), Eugenijus Ališanka has also edited this volume.

Photograph of Laima Vincė by Tony Ward; all other photographs courtesy of *The Vilnius Review*.

Other anthologies of poetry in translation
published in bilingual editions by Arc Publications
include:

Altered State: An Anthology of New Polish Poetry
EDS. ROD MENGHAM, TADEUSZ PIÓRO, PIOTR SZYMOR
Translated by Rod Mengham, Tadeusz Pióro *et al*

A Fine Line: New Poetry from Eastern
& Central Europe
EDS. JEAN BOASE-BEIER, ALEXANDRA BÜCHLER, FIONA SAMPSON
Various translators

Six Slovenian Poets
ED. BRANE MOZETIČ
Translated by Ana Jelnikar, Kelly Lennox Allen
& Stephen Watts, with an introduction by
Aleš Debeljak
NO. 1 IN THE 'NEW VOICES FROM EUROPE & BEYOND' ANTHOLOGY SERIES,
SERIES EDITOR: ALEXANDRA BÜCHLER

Six Basque Poets
ED. MARI JOSE OLAZIREGI
Translated by Amaia Gabantxo, with an introduction by
Mari Jose Olaziregi
NO. 2 IN THE 'NEW VOICES FROM EUROPE & BEYOND' ANTHOLOGY SERIES,
SERIES EDITOR: ALEXANDRA BÜCHLER

A Balkan Exchange:
Eight Poets from Bulgaria & Britain
ED. W. N. HERBERT

The Page and The Fire:
Poems by Russian Poets on Russian Poets
ED. PETER ORAM
Selected, translated and introduced by Peter Oram

Six Czech Poets
ED. ALEXANDRA BÜCHLER
Translated by Alexandra Büchler, Justin Quinn
& James Naughton, with an introduction by
Alexandra Büchler
NO. 3 IN THE 'NEW VOICES FROM EUROPE & BEYOND' ANTHOLOGY SERIES,
SERIES EDITOR: ALEXANDRA BÜCHLER